The Choice to Rejoice

*Finding joy despite
life's circumstances*

A special thanks to my wife Terry, for allowing me to spend so many evenings after work in front of a computer writing. She has walked hand in hand with me through almost forty years of ministry. Terry is a major reason for my relationship with Jesus Christ and for learning how to rejoice in the Lord despite life's circumstances.

I also want to thank our dear friend and my editor, Angie Frizzell for her diligence, patience, and encouragement. Her insight goes beyond technical expertise in developing the manuscript. She has given invaluable spiritual counsel to make this book the best it can be for the Lord.

Both helped me to make this work possible to the glory of God.

"Paul has this amazing way of actually bringing us into the mind and heart of the individual he is writing about. We feel their anguish and despair. We see these Biblical and historical characters showing their process of choosing to rejoice in the LORD through the hardest of circumstances. A must read for anyone desiring to develop character, endurance, and joy for the journey."

Ricky Sinclair, Author of Miracle at Large
Pastor of Miracle Place Church of Baker, LA.

"The Choice to Rejoice is a very practical book on how to make it when difficult times come our way. We all have faced it or will face it at some point in our life. What will we do when it comes? How will we get through it? Quitting is not an option.

This book helps to answer these questions, while giving personal experiences and how applying the Biblical truths found in God's Word can make all the difference in our lives. I believe this book will both bless and encourage the reader in the area of how to make it through challenging times."

Timmy Straight, Campus Pastor
Healing Place Church, St. Francisville, LA.

The choice to rejoice, as my dear friend, Paul Pierce points out, is not merely a cliché or cute saying but rather a choice that all believers must make almost daily if not every day of their life. Paul masterfully uses different heroes of the faith from the Bible such as Job, Joshua, Paul, David, and others to lay out the reality that every circumstance and situation we encounter does not lend itself to automatic rejoicing. Sometimes, we must choose to rejoice even when our flesh revolts against the notion entirely. Even in the face of adversity, persecution and heartache, these men of the Bible choose to rejoice. You will find comfort and encouragement through the pages of this book to follow the command of the Scripture to "REJOICE in the Lord always and again I say REJOICE." You and I, like so many before us, have a choice to make. I hope we will always, no matter the circumstances, choose to REJOICE!

Randy Frizzell, Associate Pastor/Pastoral Care
Building Church of Huntsville, AL.

Scripture taken from the NEW AMERICAN STANDARD BIBLE®, Copyright © 1960,1962,1963,1968,1971,1972,1973,1975,1977,1995 by The Lockman Foundation. Used by permission.

Scripture quotations marked NIV are taken from THE HOLY BIBLE, NEW INTERNATIONAL VERSION ®, Copyright ©1973,1978,1984,2011 by Biblica, Inc.™ Used by permission. All rights reserved.

Scripture quotations marked NLT are taken from THE HOLY BIBLE, NEW LIVING TRANSLATION, Copyright © 1996, 2004, 2015 by Tyndale House Foundation. Used by permission of Tyndale House Publishers, Inc. All rights reserved.

Scripture quotations marked KJV are taken from THE HOLY BIBLE, KING JAMES VERSION, in the public domain.

Additional copies of
The Choice to Rejoice
*may be purchased on Amazon.com.
You can order from the **Books** page on my web site,
www.transformedliving.net.
Just click on the book image on the page to be
directed to Amazon.*

*Other books I have written are listed there and
can be ordered as well.*

Transformed: Redeemed from the Fall

Extraordinary!

Scabs to Scars

Scotty Scarecrow: Afraid of the Dark

Table of Contents

Faces in the Crowd — 1

Alone in the Dark — 13

Facing Overwhelming Obstacles — 45

All is Lost — 77

Waiting for Your Destiny — 103

Deeper Revelation — 128

The Finish Line — 155

The Choice is Yours Now — 180

The Last Word — 195

Chapter 1
Faces in the Crowd

Have you ever walked through a crowded shopping mall or arena and wondered what is really going on behind the faces of the people you meet? I have looked at people as I walked through a crowd. Most people don't acknowledge my look. Some are laughing while others seem distracted. It's hard to know what a person is thinking by looking on the outside only.

Some statistics say as much as twenty percent of the population is struggling with some form of anxiety or depression at any given time. It affects young and old, male and female of every race equally. Millions struggle with minor occasional bouts of sadness, melancholy and discouragement related to life's circumstances.

I wonder when I walk through the crowd if I can pick out the one in five people who are carrying this burden. I look intently as they pass me by. All I see is faces in the crowd.

I was one of those faces for a couple of years. I struggled with despondent thoughts while continuing to be a husband, father, employee and minister. The feelings of despair and discouragement sometimes felt like the pull of a whirlpool dragging me down each day. Every day was a struggle. I will get more into my story later.

As a pastor and minister, I have been called on to pray and counsel people in all sorts of situations. I have worked with at-risk youth who were filled with anger over the rejection they felt from unconcerned parents. There were several times I was needed to pray with people who were incarcerated, or the family members affected by incarceration. I was challenged by those who looked to me for answers after the death of a child, an attempted suicide, or tragically, a successful suicide.

I remember their faces. They were normal people like anyone else who experienced something in their life that caused them to fall into despair.

A young lady came to me after being physically beaten and verbally abused by her spouse. He kicked her out of the house with nowhere to go. She went to work with the humiliation of wearing sunglasses inside the office to hide her bruised eyes.

A young family cried when trying to understand what happened. Their bundle of joy was gone because of Sudden Infant Death Syndrome (SIDS). The silence in the house was more than the two of them could bear.

A middle-aged father surrendered his firearm to me in his bedroom as he struggled against suicidal thoughts. Nothing could make him see how much he was loved by his three lovely girls. Eventually the battle was lost years later when he died at his own hands.

A young boy of twelve years lashed out in anger at everyone because of his parents' divorce. He tried to hit me out of frustration at the uncontrollable situation.

A mother screamed in denial at the loss of her daughter and two grandchildren in an apparent murder-suicide. This could not be true. Why would this beautiful young mother do something so terrible? It was unthinkable.

A young wife weeps as troopers inform her that her husband has been tragically killed in a traffic accident. It was the day before Mother's Day. He was out buying her a gift for her first Mothers' Day.

Family members walked around the hospital in a daze at the pronouncement of Stage Four cancer for a loving wife, mother, and grandmother. She was given a prognosis of days or weeks to live.

An elderly gentleman tears up as he tells me of the tragic loss of his middle-aged daughter in a tragic auto accident. He can't understand how she can die before him. It's not right or natural for a parent to out-live their child. Why would God take his beautiful daughter from her children and family?

A woman weeps as she tries to explain how Alzheimer's has stolen her mother's mind. She watches daily as the strong woman who cared for her as a child now deteriorates before her eyes.

A forty-year old man tells me of the many times he has tried to free himself of his drug addiction and failed. He is afraid to try gain and possibly fail again.

A young woman hides her face in shame. She tells of her sexual molestation as a young teen. The perpetrator was a trusted family member. Who would take the word of a kid against a grown-up? She had been using her love of food to cover her problem. Now she could no longer lose the weight.

Children from broken homes sat before me wondering what was wrong with them and why no one loved them. Their cries still ring in my ears today. Their precious broken hearts were displayed through disobedience, rebellion and fits of anger. They did not know any other way to deal with the hurt and sadness they felt every day.

Two young teens sat before me asking how they could ever explain to their parents that she is pregnant. What should she do? What about an abortion? This was not an option for them. They made a mistake but killing a baby was not the answer. How would their lives ever be the same again?

A young wife struggles with the decision to stay with her husband. He has been incarcerated again and she is left to raise her two young boys alone. How could she tell them their father was not coming home?

An older pastor cried in front of me when I was a college student. He knew he could express his pain and sorrow to us, four young visiting preachers. We would be off to the next church engagement tomorrow and he would carry on alone. No one in the church would know his struggle and despair.

A man tried to explain his loss for words when his wife of many years confessed her infidelity to him. He wanted reconciliation, but she was already gone.

Overdoses too many to count. Traffic fatalities in the dozens. Divorces and separations tearing families to shreds. Parents losing their children to addiction. Children watching their parents or grandparents suffer from the terrible effects of years of smoking or drinking. Men and women trying to find a way to tell their spouses they lost their job and may soon lose everything else.

It's no wonder people are depressed. It might be easier to help if we wore signs around our necks proclaiming our struggles. That will never happen. We look into the smiling faces of hurting people and they never know we feel the same.

Our pride keeps us from admitting we struggle. Sometimes we continue until it is too late. We hide it behind the "masks" we call our face. Every race, both sexes and all ages are affected by anxiety, fear, and despair.

I have spent most of my adult life trying to help people find hope. I understand some of the challenges we face. Sometimes these are emotional expressions of anxiety or despondency that will pass. Other people face a daily struggle that is persistent and powerful. The causes may be physical, emotional, social, or spiritual.

God created us as body, soul, and spirit. Many times, the causes are a combination of causes and compounded by frustration and fear. That is why this phenomenon is so difficult to understand. It is even more difficult to treat and see a person return to a full productive life.

I don't want to appear to know more than physicians, psychologists, psychiatrists or other mental health professionals. I am not purporting myself to be an expert in theology or biblical instruction. I have enough training in the areas of counseling to recognize how little I really know.

I am a lot like the blind man in the Gospel of John: *He replied, "Whether He (Jesus Christ) **is** a sinner or not, I don't know. One thing I do know. **I was blind but now I see!**"*[1]

I have experienced the dark times of discouragement, despair, and despondency. I have struggled through sleepless nights with thoughts in my mind that would not stop. I have worried that people would discover that I was faking as a Christian and pastor because of my struggles. I have been through days of anger and hopelessness. I was one of those faces in the crowd, but not any longer. Now I see!

I discovered a powerful weapon in my personal fight against darkness and depression. I learned that God

---

[1] John 9:25 NIV

has given dozens of scriptures and stories of other people in the Bible who struggled just like me.

Some of the great characters of the Bible like King David of Israel, Job, the Prophet Elijah suffered through those same sleepless nights. The great New Testament preachers, Peter and Paul also had their times of discouragement and depression. Their status as people of God did not make them less disheartened.

The reasons for their experiences were as varied as ours today. The feelings and emotions were the same. Their struggles to overcome anxiety and doubt helped me see that there is an answer. If I could only find the secret!

Hopefully, this book will provide some light for you if you find yourself, or someone you love, like one of those faces in the crowd.

Read on if you are like I was at that time – desperate, depressed, alone, discouraged by the past and afraid of the future. These stories will give you hope again.

You will learn the power of The Choice to Rejoice, too. God will change your life even if the circumstances never change. He gave us all the power to choose. It's time to choose.

Chapter 2

Alone in the Dark

The frigid air smelled of death and rotting flesh, making it almost impossible to breathe. Foul water gurgled noisily down the walls from the path above. An angry outburst of cursing from somewhere in the darkness drowned out the flowing moans and groans of broken men.

Cold shackles rubbed flesh raw at the wrists and ankles of the two newest prisoners. Their bodies screamed with bruises and cuts from the beating inflicted on them. Fire seemed to leap from the open cuts as the vinegar splashed on them. The blood flowing from their wounds ran red upon the ground. Physical torture was more than a skill. It became a sadistic art form for the Roman centurions. They took pleasure in inflicting pain. The entire world both revered and reviled them for their expertise.

Silence finally enveloped the normal haunting cries of the jail. Singing could be heard from the deepest bowels of that dank hole. Prisoners young and old lifted their weary bedraggled heads as they listened to the two new members. It started out low and soft but soon became boisterous and loud. Even the routine shouts of anger and pain were drowned out. Everyone but these two weary prisoners became silent. All were astounded by joy and praises that flowed from that cell throughout the whole prison.

Many nights a prison melody echoed through the jail. The song usually expressed pain, grief, and sorrow, but this was different. These two men were not singing their sorrows but were expressing praise to the Living God. It was startling and amazing!

"The Lord is in this place" ... "He has never forsaken" ... "He is my song and my deliverer." Paul and Silas sang as loudly as their weakened bodies would allow. Locked in stocks hand and foot, all they could do was sing, but their voices reverberated through the entire prison! No one dared make a sound while the two of them praised the Lord God, Jehovah for hours.

The songs began to fade as the two men finally tired. Weeping could be heard through the quietness from other parts of the damp darkness. Suddenly, the dark prison exploded in the brightness of the glory of God! The quaking walls and floor groaned loudly beneath the power of the Lord. Dungeon doors flew open and the chains and stocks miraculously burst from the hands of Paul & Silas.

All through the jail, metal creaked and squealed as prison doors burst opened. The guard raced to slam them closed as fast as they opened. Chaos erupted everywhere as the centurion shouted above the den. With his sword drawn, he stepped menacingly to the forefront of the crowd. Prisoners cowered back against the walls in fear. While they watched, he collapsed to his knees and placed the sword to his abdomen. Some of the prisoners cheered as great drops of perspiration flowed down his contorted face.

"Stop, don't harm yourself or anyone else! We are all here." The shout from the darkness suddenly both shocked and stopped everyone in their tracks. Silence filled the dungeon like a flood of waters. Paul and Silas worked their way through the throng to the centurion as the other prisoners gathered around them.

The large hulking soldier was on his knees on the cold stone floor. His cheeks were wet with the stinging mixture of perspiration and tears. Despair contorted his face as he contemplated taking his life. His life was over anyway once his failure was discovered by command.

As Paul approached him, his face displayed a mind racing with conflicting thoughts. He was normally so sure of himself. The fear that gripped his soul was squeezing the breath from his lungs. Flaming arrows from unseen enemies in darkness had not shaken him like this moment. He realized that he was facing something greater than he ever imagined. Only God could unlock prison doors and chains with such miraculous power.

Massive forearms trembled as sweat trickled down the guard's arm. His knuckles where whitened from his death grip on the sword. The gentle touch of Paul's hand on his shoulder startled and stiffened him. He pulled back as a warning to the unwanted

Paul's eyes shined with so much compassion toward this man, it melted his stone heart. The soldier began to weep. This battle-hardened soldier who never cried now wept uncontrollably. Shame he felt for the life he lived was greater than any battlefield fear he ever experienced.

Overwhelming guilt for his own wretchedness came flooding from his soul. The tears cascaded from his cheeks and puddled on the floor. His massive shoulders lurched under the burden of his sin.

God's holy presence filled the atmosphere of the dark dungeon in that moment of quiet stillness. Angry screams from other prisoners had changed to weeping from the realization of their own sinfulness. Deep groans of grief replaced the moans of suffering.

Paul slipped his hand over the cold steel blade and gently pulled it away. Silas slipped his aching swollen arms around the massive man, lifting him from his knees. He wrapped him tightly as blood still dripped from his wounds.

The centurion buried his face into Silas' chest. The two men stood there weeping together. The power of the Lord was visibly shaking the two men. The locked door to the heart of this man of war was opened just like the jail cells had flown open only a few minutes earlier.

After a few moments, Paul lightly separated the two men from their embrace. Every wound in his body screamed in agony as he looked into the jailer's mahogany brown face muddied with tears. This broken man dared not look the man of God in the eyes.

Summoning all of his strength, he lifted his head to speak. With trembling, the sobbing centurion's voice broke the silence. "Sirs, what must I do to be saved?"

I have never spent a day inside a physical prison, but I have felt the chains of discouragement and fear close around me during the night. Many of us have gone through experiences in life that are overwhelming.

Paul and Silas, two missionaries and early leaders in the New Testament church, are tremendous examples to every believer. Their lives were polarizing in the times in which they lived. They were committed disciples of Christ and bold preachers of the gospel. Each of the men gave powerful testimony to the grace of God in their lives.

Many days and nights were spent traveling from one village to another. Sometimes they were well received in the cities they visited. On more than a few occasions, people were waiting for their arrival. Opposition to the gospel was strong but there were always those curious to hear this new message.

Paul was known by reputation around the regions of Asia Minor. His other missionary journeys had brought him to major cities of Antioch, Iconium, Lystra, and Derbe. This was the first opportunity for the gospel to be presented in Macedonia.

On their second missionary journey, Paul and Silas wanted to confirm the works of the first journey of Paul and Barnabas. The plan was to visit each of the churches established on that first trip. Then, as the Lord gave opportunity, they would expand into new areas.

One of the most unusual passages of scripture describes what happened during this journey. Paul and Silas went back through Lystra and Iconium. There they added a young disciple named Timothy to their group.

Next Paul and Silas traveled through the area of Phrygia and Galatia because the Holy Spirit had prevented them from preaching the word in the province of Asia at that time. Then coming to the borders of Mysia, they headed north for the province of Bithynia, but again the Spirit of Jesus did not allow them to go there. So instead, they went on through Mysia to the seaport of Troas.

How strange that God would prevent these men from doing the very task assigned to them. The Spirit of God stopped them from moving forward into the areas of Phrygia, Galatia, and Bithynia. It is an awesome thing that these men were so in tune with the Spirit that they knew when to stop.

Paul received a vision from God during the night that gave them direction for the mission. A man of Macedonia appeared to him with a message. "Come over and help us." After discussion, the missionaries decided this was God's directive to take the gospel to the area now known as Greece. They proceeded with joy. Their hearts raced as they thought of being the first to preach the gospel in those regions.

Their journey took them to the major city of Macedonia at that time, Philippi. It was a coastal city, a large metropolis and Roman colony. Here they would preach the gospel for the first time in the country of Greece.

Their first converts were god-fearing people who received them openly. A merchant woman from the city of Thyatira received the message of Christ with joy. She invited all those in her family to join her. They welcomed the missionary team into their home in Philippi.

The trouble began in a peculiar way. There was a young girl who was a fortune teller and under the influence of demonic spirits. The spirit inside her recognized the Holy Spirit's presence in the visiting preachers. Spiritual darkness cannot ever overpower the light of Jesus in a believer.

The scriptures say this evil spirit in the girl caused her to follow the missionaries and persistently attack them. Day after day, she screamed at them and announced to all around these men were here to bring salvation. Everywhere they went, she created a spectacle.

Sometimes the devil's tactics just do not make sense. Suddenly, Paul was at his limit of patience. In exasperation, he cast the demon out of the girl. She was in her right mind instantly.

There is no explanation why Paul did not cast the demon out sooner. It is certain that the power to do so was there all along. Evil spirits respond to authority in the Jesus name. They are not moved by frustration exposed in his followers. These two men had cast out many other demons in their time of ministry. Why not now?

It is possible, Paul and the others ascertained that this action might hinder their work in Philippi. Maybe they had been warned by well-meaning people not to do this. Since no reason is given in explanation, then speculation is all we have.

Sometimes doing the right thing is difficult. Much of modern Christian teaching today says if we obey God, our lives will be full of blessing. Those blessings are defined as riches, health, and popularity. Following Christ is presented as a way to prosperity and happiness. This is not exactly correct.

Paul was obeying his direct commission and following the example of Christ. He was in this place by divine leadership. As far as we can tell, the Spirit of God inside Paul and the evangelists was provoking this evil spirit. The power of the gospel was dispelling darkness as surely as a lit candle lights a darkened room. Paul was doing the right thing in the right place in the right way.

This great act of deliverance was not celebrated. Those who lost their means of profit from the demonic gift in the girl became angry. Grabbing the leaders, these men dragged Paul and Silas before the magistrates. A crowd gathered to support their cries for justice. The court ordered Paul & Silas beaten and imprisoned. The guard was threatened with death if they escaped.

Once in the prison, the guard had them placed in the deepest part of the prison. Their hands and feet were locked in stocks and their bodies chained to the wall. Then the door was slammed shut while they suffered from the beating.

Large men rained down hails of blows with wooden rods upon their exposed backs. Each soldier took his turn in an attempt to inflict more pain than the previous one. They laughed and jeered at one another as the two missionaries persevered the torture.

To most of us, this would seem to be a daunting place. Most of us will never endure physical cruelty at the hands of evil people. Being locked up unjustly for simple obedience to Christ seems foreign. Separation and isolation from friends in darkness can be unbearable.

It was a dark time for the two evangelists. Maybe the questions flooded their mind as they sat in jail. "Why did this happen to us, Lord?" "What did we do wrong?" "How long will we be here?" "How can this be part of Your plan for us Lord?" I am sure these would be my thoughts.

You have been there. Maybe you have never experienced physical torture and imprisonment. You have experienced fear and pain and suffering. There have been times your heart was gripped with sorrow and depression. You have felt trapped in a situation with no resolution in sight. You have wondered "Where are you Lord?" Confusion flooded your thoughts like storm clouds. We have all been there.

Sometimes the real question is "What do I do now?" Serious stuff happens to us all. No one is immune to tragedy or difficulty. One minute the sun seems to be shining on your life then the storms blow in without warning. Jesus even warned about this very thing.

What happens to us is not as important as how we respond. That is the core principle of the Choice to Rejoice. When the doctor says the dreaded prognosis "Cancer", what do we do? How do we respond to the tragic loss of a child in a traffic accident? Who will we call when the police are wanting to search our child's belongings at school? What will people think of us as a Christian when news gets out? What will we say when someone accuses us falsely and it results in the loss of our job and home?

The list can go on endlessly. The feelings of being trapped and alone we experience when these things happen are similar to Paul and Silas in that prison. Invisible bars of fear, worry, depression, and bitterness keep us locked up on the inside. All joy in living is lost.

It seems like these feelings are exaggerated when it is dark, and we are alone. It is hard to see a way out. One story about Christ and his disciples illustrates this situation. After ministering to crowds, the men following Jesus entered a boat with Him. After a while on the water, darkness of night was compounded by the clouds of a terrible storm.

I have been on the water in a small boat in a situation like this. The horizon disappears into blackness. Storms batter the boat and it seems like little or no progress is made against the wind. It is hard to see land or anything else. The disciples began to cry out, "Lord, where are you? Don't you care that we are about to die?"

Paul and Silas could have felt the same way. We do not know how they felt. We do know how they acted. In the midst of their darkest hour, they praised God. They lifted up their voices declaring the goodness and greatness of God in spite of their present situation. They made a choice to rejoice.

These are four lessons or principles to learn from this story. If you will put these into practice in your life, you will experience new freedom and a strengthening to your faith.

Acknowledge God's Plan

Sometimes it can be difficult to understand that our present situation is part of the plan of God. Some things are by His design. Others are by His permission. All things that happen to the believer are used by the Lord to transform us into the image of Christ. This is His ultimate plan for us as believers.

If we allow confusion about God's love and faithfulness to us, it is possible to miss out on the lesson He wants us to learn. Sometimes our personal dreams and desires cloud the issue. It is easy to fall into the trap of believing God is blessing what we are doing instead of doing what God is blessing. We can easily miss Him.

God is good. He is faithful. He is loving and compassionate towards all mankind, even to those who resist and reject Him. Because He is over all things, He can see the end of a thing from the beginning. His view is much clearer than our own puny understanding.

Sometimes God's plan is so much greater than just our own personal safety and comfort. He may be using situations in our life to teach us more about His grace and reach others with that grace at the same time. It is a step of faith and a sign of maturity to acknowledge God is in control even when it feels like He is not. When we do not understand the plan, we simply must trust His heart. God is faithful and good.

Be Aware of God's Presence

It is easy to miss God's presence in the midst of our dark times. Just like the disciples on the boat, we can know Jesus is here but still not feel His presence. The Lord has said, "I will be with you in trouble." He does not lie but sometimes we do not feel like he is there.

Trusting in feelings is a tricky thing. Emotions can be deceiving. The fact the disciples did not feel His presence in the boat did not negate the fact Jesus was with them. He was right there undisturbed by the very situation we cannot comprehend. He knew His purpose was not completed so fear had no place in His mind.

Acknowledging God's plan for His life gave Jesus great peace. It allowed Him to experience the presence of His Father when others doubted. He knew God was with Him.

We must train our minds to respond to the Spirit rather than the flesh. The natural response to adverse situations is anger, doubt, confusion, and fear. We must choose to see God working in our behalf. We need to spend enough time with Him, to recognize His work in our life when it comes. We need to hear His voice.

I remember a day when my youngest daughter and I were driving to the church. The two-lane road we were on had a large curve preceding a railroad crossing. A slight misty rain was falling. As I approached the curve, I heard the voice of the Lord in my heart say, "Slow down."

I know some people may think it strange that I say God spoke to me. I did not hear an audible voice in the car, but I recognize when He is speaking to me. Sometimes it is through an image and other times through a thought. The Bible says "My sheep hear my voice, and I know them, and they follow me:" I have learned to recognize when the Lord is speaking to me.

Knowing He is speaking is important but responding to His voice is what He desires. As I approached the curve, I heard Him speak. I took my foot off the gas pedal allowing the car to begin slowing. My natural mind thought about sliding off the wet road in the curve with my daughter in the car. My wife would never let me live that down.

As we came around the curve, suddenly a freight train blew through the intersection. I had just enough time to stop the van before hitting the train. I think my daughter shouted in fear as the train blasted past her door. It becomes a little cloudy as I sat there in shock at what happened.

We would have been killed if I had not slowed down. We need to understand God is present with us always, not just when we are in church. He is always speaking. He is always watching over us. At times, He is protecting even when we do not have a clue.

Act on God's Prescription

So what do we do? How do we respond in the tough times? That is the test. God allows us to make the choices. The decision we make either stops or allows God to work in our behalf.

The following verses can give us a clue to how we can respond to the troubles we face.

Job stood up and tore his robe in grief. Then he shaved his head and fell to the ground to worship. He said, "I came naked from my mother's womb, and I will be naked when I leave. The LORD gave me what I had, and the LORD has taken it away. Praise the name of the LORD!" In all of this, Job did not sin by blaming God. [2]

I will praise thee, O Lord, with my whole heart; I will shew forth all thy marvelous works. I will be glad and rejoice in thee: I will sing praise to thy name, O thou most High.[3]

---

[2] Job 1:20,21
[3] Psalm 9:1,2 NASB

The LORD is my strength and my shield; my heart trusted in him, and I am helped: therefore, my heart greatly rejoices; and with my song will I praise him.[4]

Then I will rejoice in the LORD. I will be glad because he rescues me. With every bone in my body I will praise him: "LORD, who can compare with you? Who else rescues the helpless from the strong? Who else protects the helpless from those who rob them?"[5]

I waited patiently for the LORD; and he inclined unto me and heard my cry. He brought me up also out of a horrible pit, out of the miry clay, and set my feet upon a rock, and established my goings. And he hath put a new song in my mouth, even praise unto our

---

[4] Psalm 28:7 NASB
[5] Psalm 35:9,10 NIV

God: many shall see it, and fear, and shall trust in the LORD. [6]

Why are you in despair, O my soul? Why have you become restless and disquieted within me? Hope in God and wait expectantly for Him, for I shall yet praise Him, The help of my countenance and my God. [7]

I am suffering and in pain. Rescue me, O God, by your saving power. Then I will praise God's name with singing, and I will honor him with thanksgiving. For this will please the LORD more than sacrificing cattle, more than presenting a bull with its horns and hooves. [8]

Praise the LORD! Let all that I am praise the LORD. I will praise the LORD as long as I live. I will sing

---

[6] Psalm 40:1-3 NASB
[7] Psalm 42:5 NASB
[8] Psalm 69:29,30 NASB

praises to my God with my dying breath. Do not put your confidence in powerful people; there is no help for you there. [9]

It is easy to say Praise the Lord! It is another thing to really praise Him and mean it when the chips are down. Paul and Silas were singing through their pain. They rejoiced in the opportunity to experience God's grace in their jail cell.

God did the impossible when they did what was possible. There were no classroom lessons on how to respond to this type of adversity. This kind of praise rolls freely only off the lips of the one who sincerely knows their God. It comes from the heart that is assured God is in control no matter how bad circumstances may appear.

---

[9] Psalm 146:1-3 NASB

Access God's Power

When we decide to offer up this spontaneous worship, God shows up. The choice is made in the natural. The results are supernatural.

The way out of your dungeon is up. If you struggle with fear or anxiety, praise the Lord in spite of your feelings! If the strong bars of depression have you locked down, turn the music up loud and shout His name. It worked for Paul and Silas. It worked for me when I was struggling in depression years ago.

I could choose to wallow in self-pity and suffer in silence. Sometimes I did just that. Then one day I decided to make a different choice. These are the principles I learned through those days. Every day I had a fresh opportunity. I could choose to rejoice in the Lord or remain in my prison of fear and depression.

The Choice to Rejoice opened the doors of my invisible jail cell and God set me free! His power can set you free too. It is time to sing His praises at the top of your lungs!

Rejoice in the Lord always, and again I say rejoice. (Paul writing to his friends in Philippi while under house arrest in Rome. Philippians 4:4)

The Pilgrim

The Pilgrim's Progress is one of the greatest books in all of English literature. It is the allegorical story of Christian, a person representing everyman. It is one of the most widely published and read books of all time. People around the globe throughout centuries since it was published have been challenged and changed by the struggles described in the story of Christian.

The story is told from the perspective of a narrator's dream. It covers Christian's travels from his home in the City of Destruction, where his burdens strapped to his back will eventually drag him into Hell, to the Celestial City on Mount Zion

John Bunyan wrote this amazing story from his prison cell. He was a Baptist minister in England at a time when only licensed Anglican ministers were allowed to preach. The King of England sat as head of the Anglican Church in England, so his wishes became the law of the land. John refused to stop preaching of the grace of God because he did not have permission of the government at that time.

John Bunyan was born in the small village of Elstow near Bedford in 1628. He spent his early years serving in the army and working as a tinker.

John would confess in his other writings that during these youthful years he was the ringleader of the worst crowd of sinners. He had little to do with religion or God. His life was that of everyman in his allegory.

After he married, John was influenced by his wife to attend services. He read two books she offered him that changed his course of life. She was Evangelist that directed him down the Strait Path to deliverance. After a few years, he moved his family to join the non-conformist Puritan congregation called the Bedford Free Church.

Under the leadership of Oliver Cromwell, England had experienced freedom to practice religion as a course of conscience. Once he lost power and the monarchy was restored under King Charles II in 1660, those protections were lost. It was then that Bunyan was forced to choose personal freedom or spiritual freedom

He spent twelve years in prison for his convictions. Even when offered his freedom if he stopped his unlawful preaching, Bunyan replied, "Release me today and tomorrow I will preach."

John produced two of his greatest works while incarcerated. His autobiography, <u>Grace Abounding to the Chief of Sinners,</u> was the first. <u>The Pilgrim's Progress</u> was written over the course of two different imprisonments.

During his life, John Bunyan was faced with serious hardships. His young wife cared for his four children without him or a steady means of provision. Still he could not surrender his call from God to preach the goodness of His grace.

There is no way to quantify the significance of his time in prison. He may have written the books if he was free but the fact that he did it while separated from everything dear in his life is powerful. Prison doors of sin and its destruction were opened for millions of "everymen" through the life of the Pilgrim. John truly made the choice to rejoice in spite of his circumstances.

Chapter 3
Facing Overwhelming Obstacles

The Commander stood alone outside the camp. As the evening sky chased the sun beyond the horizon, he looked over the massive walls of Jericho. Rustling leaves accompanied the sound of babbling waters of the nearby Jordan river.

How many nights had he spent alone overlooking his enemy positions before a battle? This one felt different. It was the first time he would be on the sidelines as his generals led the men. It would be the first battle without Moses lifting him up to the Lord.

The stone walls seemed to rise like mountainous plateaus from the earth. Lights from within the apartments built inside the massive barriers illuminated the open plain. His people would be completely exposed to enemy forces as they approached Jericho.

A noise in the brush behind him startled Joshua back from his thoughts. He spun around hand gripping his sword at his side. His arms bulged as muscles tightened in preparation for drawing the heavy blade.

The figure of a man under a tree limb was barely visible in the dusky haze. Was he friend or foe? No one from the camp knew he was here. If the enemy had found him, he would be all alone. Wedging his feet deeper into the sandy soil, Joshua readied himself for battle.

Moments passed like hours as the two men stared at one another across the moonlit field. "Are you for us or for our adversaries?" Joshua's voice was strong and firm. His eyes keenly surveyed his surroundings to catch a glimpse of other possible combatants.

When the man finally answered, his words rolled like the rumble of falling waters. Joshua was startled by the reply as much as he was by the voice. "No, I am here as captain of the army of the Lord."

Joshua fell to his knees. He bowed himself low to the ground in reverence. He was in the Presence.

The time on Mount Sinai with Moses and the many days serving in the tabernacle made Joshua awfully familiar with the Presence. The Lord Jehovah revealed Himself to very few human beings. Moses was one of those favored ones and Joshua his servant.

When Moses asked God for His name so he could tell the people and Pharaoh who sent him, he was given "I am that I am." Through the years together, God had revealed Himself "I am Righteousness," "I am Healing," "I am Provider" and "I am Present."

As Joshua bowed his face to the dirt in worship, the Lord approached him. Without daring to raise his eyes in the Presence, Joshua said, "What do you want your servant to do?" The quietness sent a shiver up the spine of this great warrior like a cold draft.

The voice was closer now when He spoke. "Take off your sandals for this place is holy."

The man Joshua is not as familiar to many as Abraham, father of Israel or the great leader Moses. His importance to the fledgling nation of Israel cannot be overstated. He was a great servant, warrior, and leader. Joshua was responsible for establishing the people of Israel in the promised land after the death of Moses. Even fearless warriors are tested.

Many new Christians are surprised to find the Christian life is not as easy as it was promoted from the pulpit. We tend to talk loudly about all of the blessings to following Christ. We sometimes understate the fact that the Christian life is one of challenge and inner change. Many people who started out following Christ, when facing obstacles, become disillusioned and quit. It is sad but true.

The book of Joshua is a historical record of the journey of the Israelite people into the Promised Land under the new leadership of Joshua, son of Nun. Joshua was formerly the servant to Moses and the military leader of Israel. Now that Moses has died, Joshua has become the spiritual leader of the nation as well.

A brief summary of the life of Joshua will help us to understand better his *Choice to Rejoice* when the time arrived. Joshua son of Nun was one of the twelve tribal leaders chosen by Moses to spy out the Promised Land. Only he and Caleb, son of Jephunnah, returned from their reconnaissance with a favorable report. Their faith in God spared them from the fate of dying in the wilderness with all those who chose not to believe God.

The other ten men saw the same walled cities and obstacles as Joshua and Caleb. These ten leaders saw the same beauty and bounty of the land. They allowed fear and unbelief to overwhelm their faith. This separated them from Joshua and Caleb. Those who chose to believe their faithless evil report were doomed to wander in the wilderness. One year of wandering for each day the spies were in the Promised Land was their sentence.

Even though they were allowed to live, the two men still spent forty years in the desert with the unbelievers. They watched as all those of adult age perished in the wandering. Joshua became a singular servant to Moses, God's man. Caleb returned to lead those of his clan through the forty years of roaming the desert.

For forty days, Joshua was alone with Moses on Mount Sinai when the Lord gave the Commandments. He was closer to the Presence than any other man. The Israelites saw the cloud of God's glory from the base of the mountain while Joshua was inside the cloud with Moses.

Years later, the Israelites constructed the Tabernacle of the Presence. This was the place God dwelt over His Ark of the Presence when the Israelites stopped. Moses ministered to the Lord and received his instructions from God in this tabernacle. Only Joshua was in the tent with him. Many times, after Moses left the Presence, Joshua remained behind.

Nothing is said in scripture to tell us what happened during these times. We do know that the Presence of God was so strong, when Moses left the tent, he covered his face. The frightening glory of God shone upon him like the sun illuminates the fullest moon.

It may be conjecture, but these times shaped Joshua. His faith had opened a door for him into a unique position with the Lord. The time spent in the Presence prepared him for the days to come.

Joshua served as Moses's special minister, but he was also a mighty soldier. He was general over the armies and led the people through many conflicts and battles.

One of the most notable battles took place at Rephidim, the place where God brought water from the rock for the people. Armies of Amalek gathered to attack Israel there. The two nations met in the valley while Moses, Aaron and Hur watched atop the mountain.

Amalek prevailed against Joshua and Israel. Joshua looked to the hill where Moses stood. Moses lifted his hand to God and the power of God came on Israel to prevail. When Moses tired, he lowered his hands. Suddenly Amalek began to prevail against them. When he lifted his hands again, the Israelites prevailed.

While the battle ensued throughout the day, the struggle continued. Every time Moses lifted his hands, Israel took the upper hand. When he tired, Israel faltered. Finally, Aaron and Hur sat Moses on a rock and positioned his hands on their shoulders. As a result, the Lord empowered and enabled Joshua with Israel to obtain the victory.

The Israelites on the journey from Egypt are representative of the life of a new believer. Egypt is a parallel to the old life of bondage, like a sinner caught up in sin. The Israelites were under a cruel taskmaster who was never satisfied and constantly demanded more. Their life was not joyful and free. It was hard and they barely subsisted.

This reminds me of my days before I began to follow Christ wholeheartedly. Sin and the devil ruled my life. There was fear of death, fear of exposure, and fear of the unknown. I was in bondage under a cruel taskmaster like Israel was to Pharaoh. There was no real joy or lasting peace.

The experiences of the Israelites parallel many of the experiences of a life of faith for a believer today. Following God today is not so different from that day. Their faith looked forward to the promise of a future Savior, while our faith looks back to the finished work of Christ on the cross. Both require faith in the unseen God of grace and obedience to His Word.

These analogies are made in 1 Corinthians 10 about Israel in the wilderness under Moses' leadership.[10] Let us make a few comparisons between the experiences of Joshua and Israel to those of a believer today.

There must be a repentance from the old way of life to start the new life. Joshua and the Israelites crossed the Jordan River miraculously and then stopped to renew their covenant with God on the other side. All the circumcised men of Israel who disobeyed the Lord in the wilderness had died off. Every man in Israel except Joshua and Caleb had to be circumcised as an act of repentance, obedience, and faith in God.

The miraculous crossing of the Jordan River was symbolic of the baptism into Christ of the believer. This is not a water baptism but the total "immersion"

---

[10] 1 Corinthians 10:1-11 NLT

into the new life.[11] The Israelites were moving into new realms of belief and new tests of faith when they crossed the river on dry ground. The believer likewise faces new challenges as we move into a life of faith.

Following Christ is a life of faith that depends on obedience to the Word of God. The same was true of the Israelite nation. The only way for Israel to experience victory and receive the land promised by God was to live in total obedience to His commands through Joshua. God spoke through Joshua. He told the Israelites to prepare to move forward because they had never been this way before.

The same is true for a new follower of Christ today. Most of us as new believers struggle to hear and understand the will of God. As we obey the will we

---

[11] Galatians 3:26-28 NLT

know, God reveals more of His plan so we can continue to move forward.

This new life brought them into direct conflict with the enemy. Before the Jordan crossing, they mostly struggled with selfishness and leaving the old ways behind. Now there were real enemies who were ready to defend their land against Israel and resist the plan of God.

The enemy had to be dispossessed in the land so the people of God could possess the promise. It was their responsibility to forcibly remove these enemy nations and establish their home in that place. God would only work in their behalf to the level of their obedience and trust in Him to do it.

When a new believer turns to follow the Lord, that person is now going against the very direction of the world and the flesh. The conflict is very real. That is why the Apostle Paul described our Christian faith as spiritual warfare.[12]

The name "Jesus" is the Greek form of the name "Joshua". This is the anglicized version of the Hebrew "Yeshua", which means *"Yah (the LORD) is deliverer or salvation"*. Jesus is the Savior and Deliverer. This same is true for Joshua's role in the story. It is not a coincidence but rather a part of the plan of God. Joshua son of Nun is a shadow of Jesus the Messiah. This man who was a man like us led the people of God through internal conflict to external victory. Joshua was their spiritual leader and their deliverer. His life is a perfect type of Christ.

The odds faced by the people of God were overwhelming. This nation had lived as slaves in a foreign land for over 400 years. Generations of

---

[12] Ephesians 6:10-18 NLT

Israelites had lived in oppression and fear with no hope of freedom. These people were wanderers, not warriors. Still they were faced with overwhelming obstacles in front of them with no retreat behind them.

If you have never read the story of Joshua and the Israelite nation, or it has been a while, I encourage you to take some time to read the first six chapters of the book of Joshua. It will encourage you and also help to make this chapter more applicable to your circumstances.

Marching Orders

Let us return back to where we started the chapter. Joshua is preparing for the greatest challenge of his life, so far.

When Joshua was near the town of Jericho, he looked up and saw a man standing in front of him with sword in hand. Joshua went up to him and demanded, "Are you friend or foe?" "Neither one," he replied. "I am the commander of the LORD's army." At this, Joshua fell with his face to the ground in reverence. "I am at your command," Joshua said. "What do you want your servant to do?" The commander of the LORD's army replied, "Take off your sandals, for the place where you are standing is holy." And Joshua did as he was told.[13]

One significant aspect of this passage may be easily overlooked. Joshua was not consulting with the military leaders. He was alone when this encounter with God happened. There alone in the darkness, Joshua was waiting for his marching orders.

Many times we move into situations without clear direction from the Lord. Each challenge we face is new. Every day has new obstacles and difficulties. When we assume that we can do the same things that gave us success in the past, we set ourselves up for

---

[13] Joshua 5:13-15 NLT

failure. It is important to allow the Lord to lead and direct our steps. We need our marching orders.

It is interesting when asked "friend or foe?", the Lord does not really answer. He says, "Neither one." He is saying He is not in the middle of our situations, but He is Lord over every situation. His view from above gives Him perfect understanding of what we need to do.

There is a strategy outlined in Joshua chapter 6 that is strange, if not ludicrous. No military council would have ever come up with a plan like the one the Lord laid out for Joshua. That is the point. This was a battle the Lord was orchestrating.

All that remained for the Israelites to receive victory was obedience to the Lord and commitment to the plan. Follow the marching orders Joshua received while alone outside the enemy walls of Jericho. Nothing could stop them if they obeyed.

That sounds simple enough to do until it is you doing it.

Massive Walls

Rising up from the plains, the walls of Jericho were an intimidating sight. That was one of the intended purposes for this massive defense against attacks. Massive, impenetrable walls discouraged the weak or faint of heart.

The Lord's plan was strategic and purposeful. Jericho was centrally located in the land promised to Israel. It was a gateway city. All who would enter the land of Canaan were forced to pass Jericho. The land was secure as long as Jericho was standing.

The question is why this way? When the Israelites left Egypt under Moses, the Lord led them away from direct contact and conflict with enemies. Why couldn't they avoid Jericho and enter the land without such a conflict?

There are several good answers to the question. First, it would manifest the glory and greatness of Jehovah to His people. These were the children and grandchildren of those who failed to obey the Lord forty years previously. They needed to know that their conquest of the land did not depend on their military savvy but upon the overwhelming power of their God.

It also would establish once again that Joshua is the man chosen by God to lead His people. The miraculous crossing of the Jordan River was the beginning of his elevation in the eyes of the people. Victory over this massive obstacle would leave no room for doubt in anyone's mind who God placed in charge.

Because of its strategic location, conquering Jericho was a military necessity. Once Jericho was defeated, it would divide the northern kingdoms from those in the south. It would make it less likely that all of the enemies could join forces against the Israelites. There would be a northern campaign and another to the south.

A final reason is given in Joshua 5:

Now it came about when all the kings of the Amorites who were beyond the Jordan to the west, and all the kings of the Canaanites who were by the sea, heard how the LORD had dried up the waters of the Jordan before the sons of Israel until they had crossed, that their hearts melted, and there was no spirit in them any longer because of the sons of Israel.[14]

The walls were intended to intimidate invaders. The word of the miraculous crossing of the natural defensive barrier stole the confidence of the enemy.

---

[14] Joshua 5:1 NLT

Fear filled their hearts and minds. The demonstration of God's power shook the foundation of the people. The arrogance of the people throughout the entire land was wiped out. No one in Canaan had ever seen evidence of a God so powerful that a mighty river in flood season could be stopped so a multitude of people could cross on the dry riverbed.

The lessons for us as believers today are numerous as well. Our God works a great deliverance to bring us into the promised land of salvation. It is a miracle when anyone is born again. Crossing the river is symbolic of our entrance into the life of faith.

Each man of age was circumcised after crossing the river into enemy territory. The act of circumcision is a foreshadowing of a believer's baptism. It was an outward sign of an inward faith and commitment.

Our promised land is not a physical location. Jesus promised us life more abundant.[15] We receive eternal life but there is so much more the Lord wants us to receive and enjoy. The problem is there are enemies ready to resist our every advance. We must be intense in our resolve, strategic in our planning, and tenacious in our action to remove these enemies from our lives. Just like the Israelite nation.

We fight our own fears and failures from the past. We want our own way and selfish desires. We continue to struggle to follow the Lord completely. That is the struggle of the flesh.

There is a real adversary, the devil. Not everything that glitters is gold and not every challenge that arises in our new life is demonic. Some things may just be the circumstances of life. That said, ask Job, Paul,

---

[15] John 10:10

and Jesus Himself if the devil is real. They will tell you without a doubt he is real and has a plan to wreak havoc and destruction in your life. He is like a roaring lion seeking someone to devour.[16]

We also struggle with the desire to conform and fit in with those around us. Following the Lord in today's world is like a salmon swimming upstream against the roaring river current. The world continuously pushes against the believer and the life of faith. The entire world is going the wrong direction but sometimes it seems we are the ones on the wrong track.

Our salvation is miraculous and so is our sanctification. Theologically, these two concepts are both positional and practical for the believer. We are saved from the penalty of sin and are being saved from the power of sin every day. We have been made

---

[16] 1 Peter 5:8

the righteousness of Christ, but He still demands we walk in that righteousness daily.

The same is true of the believer's sanctification. We are declared to be holy, but we must also live in holiness. That is removal of the old ways and patterns of life to wholly follow the Lord. Driving the enemy out of our lives is a spiritual battle. It cannot be won in our own strength and wisdom. Sanctification is a process just like a military campaign.

Conquering these enemies and obstacles that seek to stop us from achieving an abundant life is a daunting task. It requires faith and determination. Learning complete dependence on God is not easy. We need our marching orders. We need a battle plan.

The Plan

The plan given to Joshua that night is revealed in Joshua chapter 6. It was both incredible and impossible to imagine. This plan could never be drawn up on a strategy board or battle map. No military college would ever attempt to teach it as a tactical procedure. It was awesome!

Now Jericho [a fortified city with high walls] was tightly closed because [of the people's fear] of the sons of Israel; no one went out or came in. ² The LORD said to Joshua, "See, I have given Jericho into your hand, with its king and the mighty warriors. ³ Now you shall march around the city, all the men of war circling the city once. You shall do this [once each day] for six days. ⁴ Also, seven priests shall carry seven trumpets [made] of rams' horns ahead of the ark; then on the seventh day you shall march around the city seven times, and the priests shall blow the trumpets. ⁵ When they make a long blast with the ram's horn, and when you hear the sound of the trumpet, all the people shall cry out with a great shout (battle cry); and the wall of the city will fall down in its place, and the people shall go up, each man [going] straight ahead [climbing over the rubble]."

It was pretty straightforward. The priests would lead the people in a silent march around the city once each day for six days in a row. Then on the seventh day, they were to circumnavigate the city six times. On the final time around, all the men were to raise a war shout and a praise celebration with trumpets blaring.

This was a massive undertaking since several thousand soldiers were walking around a walled city in coordination and quiet. The people of the city became bold and brazen as they hurled insults and spit on the walking soldiers from above. Fear was replaced with cockiness and taunting. It was probably very humbling to these brave fighting men to not respond to the taunts and jeers verbally or militarily.

There are times when walking in obedience to the Lord is daunting. It seems the task is impossible and impenetrable. The sheer immensity of some of the challenges we face can be overwhelming. Our resolve can be shaken because we do not see how the Lord will move this immense obstacle.

Sometimes we seem to be doing the same thing over and over with no results. The Israelites walked daily not really going any place, but still they walked. They were ridiculed for it. The devil will taunt us with threats and insults in our mind. We may even become a topic for conversation for people not following the Lord.

Life can become hard. The urge to quit and turn back swells up within us. It is hard to understand how this path will lead to success and abundant life. How can this aimless wandering ever bring us victory?

Joshua and the people of Israel faced these same questions and experienced similar emotions. Times may have changed but people are still people. That is why it is so important to understand that rejoicing is a choice. When the barrier is massive and the way is difficult, the only hope we have is divine assistance. When we choose to shout in victory in the face of overwhelming obstacles, God shows up and shows off!

The walls did fall that day when the people shouted. Notice the victory shout and celebration preceded the actual victory. Real faith does not react to circumstances but proactively changes those situations. God has given us the awesome ability to make choices.

Along with the ability comes the responsibility. He makes us "response-able" in the face of every adversity and challenge. Our *Choice to Rejoice* in the face of overwhelming obstacles will bring us great deliverance and victory. *O clap your hands, all ye people; shout unto God with the voice of triumph.*[17]

---

[17] Psalm 4:1 KJV

I Did Not Know His Name

On June 8, 1968, the world lost a living example of facing and defeating overwhelming obstacles. Helen Keller spent the entirety of her life striving to overcome the disabilities of total blindness and hearing loss.

After an infantile illness, her world became dark and silent from the outside. She spent the almost eighty-eight years of her life learning and teaching others how to communicate with someone who cannot speak or hear. She refused to let those massive walls intimidate or stop her from experiencing joy in this life. She made the choice to rejoice in her circumstances.

Her governess and friend, Anne Sullivan, travelled the world alongside Helen in search of answers to their dilemma. She became Helen's teacher and greatest encourager. Persistence, challenging work and faith made it possible for Helen to learn sign language and even to speak. With her patient assistance, Helen became a renowned lecturer, activist and author who inspired people around the globe.

Her speeches and books still bring wonder and inspiration to us even today. The choices she made to press forward in spite of discouragement, fear, and resistance have opened the door for many to follow.

The Rector of Trinity Church in Boston and lyricist of *Oh Little Town of Bethlehem*, Phillips Brooks introduced Helen to Christianity at an early age. He told her of the love of God. She told the pastor, "I always knew He was there, but I didn't know his name."

Quotations by Helen:

Vision
"It is a terrible thing to see and have no vision."

Suffering
"Although the world is full of suffering, it is full also of the overcoming of it."

Persistence
"While they were saying it could not be done, it was done."

Death
"Death is no more than passing from one room into another. But there is a difference for me, you know. Because in that other room I shall be able to see."

Optimism
"Keep your face to the sun and you will never see the shadows."

Purpose
"I thank God for my handicaps. For through them, I have found myself, my work and my God."

Perseverance
"A bend in the road is not the end of the road...Unless you fail to make the turn."

Open Doors
"When one door of happiness closes, another opens; but often we look so long at the closed door that we do not see the one which has been opened for us."

Overcoming Obstacles
"Be of good cheer. Do not think of today's failures, but of the success that may come tomorrow. You have set yourselves an arduous task, but you will succeed if you persevere; and you will find a joy in overcoming obstacles. Remember, no effort that we make to attain something beautiful is ever lost."

Faith
"For three things I thank God every day of my life: thanks that he has vouchsafed me knowledge of his works; deep thanks that he has set in my darkness the lamp of faith; deep, deepest thanks that I have another life to look forward to--a life joyous with light and flowers and heavenly song."

Suffering
"Although the world is full of suffering, it is full also of the overcoming of it."

Happiness
"Happiness does not come from without, it comes from within"

Chapter 4
All is Lost

The sun burst through the curtains of the palatial hall. A servant appeared through the open door out of breath and shaking. His face carried the weight of a burden he did not want.

The master motioned him forward to speak. He made quick work of crossing the great room with large hurried strides. Sweat drops rolled from his brow. The master's wife sat up with full attention as the man began his report.

"Your oxen were plowing, with the donkeys feeding beside them, when the Sabeans raided us. They stole all the animals and killed all the farmhands. I am the only one who escaped to tell you."

Before the master could begin to question the man, another servant appeared at the entrance. There was the strong odor of smoke and burnt flesh coming from his clothing. He too was burdened and afraid to speak his news.

Rising from his table, the master motioned to this servant to speak. He stood motionless there as he received yet another terrible report.

"The fire of God has fallen from heaven and burned up your sheep and all the shepherds. I am the only one who escaped to tell you."

The shock of this report caused his wife to stand and clutch her husband by the arm. Searching his face for some sign of an answer, she waited for him to respond. His faith always carried him through every situation. He would know what to say.

Before he could reply, two servants appeared through the opening at simultaneously. Both were panting and out of breath. Their clothing was tattered. The older one was bleeding from an open wound on his arm. He spoke first.

"Three bands of Chaldean raiders have stolen your camels and killed your servants. There are none left. I alone one escaped to tell you."

The mistress struggled visibly with this terrible news. The horror of these reports took all words from her. She fell feebly back into her seat. Her breath ran away from her as she wept.

The master said nothing but looked at the younger servant. This man the master knew well. Jochabed was steward over his eldest son's household. He stood there before his master with quivering lips. Tears and perspiration encrusted by the layer of dust on his face.

"Your sons and daughters were feasting in their oldest brother's home. Suddenly, a fierce wind swept in from the wilderness and hit the house on all sides. The house collapsed." Hesitating for a moment, he continued, *"All your children are dead. I am the only one who escaped to tell you."*

A scream of agony that can only come from a mother who has lost her most precious gift resounded throughout the magnificent hall. The father who had been still suddenly and violently ripped his fabulous robe. His shredded clothing exposed his heaving chest. Anguish of soul forced its way from his lungs into a groaning never heard before in that hall. The great master fell to his knees. Gradually he lowered his head to the dusty floor. For what seemed an eternity, no other word was spoken.

Three young attendant girls came to aid their mistress. Her sobs were irrepressible. Her small frame shook with every grieving breath. No one could console her.

Finally, the master of the house calmed. Job raised himself from the dusty floor. His torn robes revealed a linen undergarment through the ripped fabric. Wiping the tears from his eyes and spittle from his beard with the sleeve of his robe, he stood there tall.

Job surveyed the room despondently. All of the servants were weeping and forlorn. When they noticed he was risen, they stopped and arose to their feet. Each one stood attentively waiting for instructions. Finally the master spoke.

"I came naked from my mother's womb, and I will be naked when I leave. The LORD gave me all I had, and the LORD has taken it away. Praise the name of the LORD!"

He gently lifted his wife from the couch and embraced her. Job held her by the shoulders and silently walked with her into his prayer sanctum. There they knelt and offered prayers and worship to the Lord.

The legend of this man Job is a true story. His life is a great instance of enduring unbelievable grief and agony. Very few people have ever experienced the loss of all in such a brief period of time. He is also an exemplary character who finds ultimate consolation in the Lord God regardless of his demise.

There are four separate episodes displayed in the story of Job and his family. The first three are the challenges faced by Job. The fourth stage is his triumphant return in the end. These are analogous to experiences to many of us as well. The challenges and lessons learned by Job may help us. We too may discover the possibility of rejoicing in the midst of losing all.

Many people assume that when troublesome events happen to other people, it is because that person has somehow brought it on themselves. There must be a cause for the effect, therefore it is supposed that person has done something wrong. Any soul experiencing such trouble has obviously sinned and deserves what is ensuing (It is peculiar how the same logic does not apply in their own life when trouble comes knocking on their particular door.)

There are times this may be true. The way of the sinner is hard.[18] There are consequences to choices

---

[18] Proverbs 13:15 KJV

that are sometimes immediate and shocking. Sometimes, there is a long delay between the decision and the result. Job was declared righteous and a man of faith by God himself. That was not why he and his wife were suffering.

Sometimes we experience troubles because of a relationship we experience. Children of all ages go through unspeakable trials when parents decide to divorce. Fighting, arguing, and manipulating one another has caused wounds that may not ever really heal. The child did nothing wrong but has to deal with the carnage.

I know many parents who have been pulled into turmoil because their children made a wrong decision. Becoming pregnant as a result of pre-marital sex is one of those common issues. Addiction to drugs, gambling and pornography also have brought financial, physical, emotional, and spiritual stress to loving parents.

Sometimes these parents did everything possible to rear their children correctly. Still, kids have a mind of their own and sometimes found themselves in situations they never anticipated or planned. Because of the connection with their children, when the child is struggling it can pull the parents into the mud along with them.

There are times when rain is just rain and a storm just a storm. Jesus said that the Lord causes His sun to shine on both just and unjust alike. The same is true of the rain. Sometimes struggle is just a part of life.

That brings us to the experience of this man named Job. He endured tribulation beyond the comprehension of most of us. Satan was given permission to sift his life in order to demonstrate his commitment to God. He went through three separate tests.

Many have asked, "Why would God allow someone who serves Him and loves Him to go through so much grief and loss?" Jesus was once asked a similar question by his followers about a man who was born blind. The disciples asked if it was the man's personal sin or the sins of his parents that caused his blindness. There had to be someone to blame for something as seriously wrong as this.

Jesus responded, *"Neither this man nor his parents sinned, but this happened so that the works of God might be displayed in him."*[19] There was no blame for his blindness. It was an opportunity for Jesus to show this man the love of God. He could also demonstrate God's power to others. Some criticized Him while others chose to believe in Him. The one born blind rejoiced. That is a common refrain throughout the Gospel accounts of the miraculous works of God.

Job's experiences were also a demonstration of God. His faithfulness to the Lord was denunciated by the enemy, Satan. Job was accused of serving God only for favor and blessings. Remove that favor and take

---

[19] John 9:1-3 NIV

away the blessings. Then it will reveal the real intent of Job's heart. The entire world will see and know that the great man of God, Job, is only serving God because of personal gain. This was the devil's dare.

God was not compelled to take up Satan's challenge. He chose to allow Job to experience tragedy as a means to reveal the glory of the Lord once again. There are some things that can only be disclosed through the fires of testing. The Lord knows our hearts better than we know ourselves. Sometimes He allows tests to reveal things in us and to us.

Trial

The first incident Job experienced was a trial of losing everything. In a few short moments Job was reduced from prosperous to pauper. He lost his oxen, donkeys, sheep, and camels in a few short moments. The hired servants were killed or taken hostage. He lost it all. His wealth and his family ruined in one stroke of circumstance.

Sometimes our possessions possess us more than we do them. The loss of everything is devastating. It brings fear and doubt for the future. It is easy to say how we would respond if it has never happened to us.

Job was not the first man to lose everything. He was the first to lose everything in such extraordinary ways. Even the loss of his personal wealth did not cause him to lose faith in God.

When we understand that we are not the source of our wealth, power, or prestige, it can be easier when it is all taken away. The reason we sometimes struggle with this trial of our faith is we have not wholly trusted the Lord in the area of provision. We may think we have created our wealth through our own creativity and effort. The loss of it all can make us feel weak and powerless.

Our accumulation of stuff can become a major source of status. Keeping up with the Joneses it is not such a new thing. We can allow our possessions to define us. This is not limited to the super-rich. Many people who struggle from paycheck to paycheck are more consumed by possessions than wealthy people. A boat or a car can become a source of personal esteem. The loss of things can be devastating when those things are allowed to control us.

Job demonstrated the proper perspective. He understood the Lord was his source of supply and that wealth was a blessing. He was not confused or controlled by his possessions. Even in the face of complete financial devastation, Job made The Choice to Rejoice in the Lord. He passed phase one of the test – trials.

Tragedy

The next phase of this attack upon Job was much more personal and tragic. After the servants reported the loss of all his possessions, the worst news any parent can receive was delivered. All his seven sons and three daughters were killed in a most horrific way. As they dined and fellowshipped in the home of the oldest brother, a terrible wind came and destroyed the house with all who were inside.

The wind came from all sides. There was no escape. There as complete destruction of the house and all within its walls. Only the steward of the house was delivered from the disaster.

His was the unwelcomed task of bringing news of the tragedy to Job and his wife. No loss of possessions can compare to the death of even one child, much less all ten in one dreadful event.

The loss of a child is the most heart-breaking experience for any parent to imagine. Most of us assume our children will outlive us. We look forward to watching them become responsible adults as we grow old. The grandchildren produced are a source of unending joy and pleasure.

Many of the funeral services I have performed have been for parents who have lost children. As a father of five children, any way a child may die is a tragic event. Sudden Infants Death Syndrome (SIDS) has been the culprit that has robbed a mother and father many times. Traffic accidents have claimed the lives of many children and young adults to whom I have ministered. These things have sadly touched even my own family.

Another dreadful experience I have encountered is adolescent suicide. The questions that plague the thoughts of a parent who has lost a child to suicide are enumerable and unanswerable. No parent wants to think their child was suffering so much that he or she felt the only way out of their turmoil was to take their own life. It takes tragic to another level.

Job lost his wealth and possessions first. Now he lost the ones most precious to him. He lost his present joy. Children can be our greatest joy and our biggest challenge simultaneously. He loved his children immensely. He prayed for them faithfully. They were his passion and concern. He wanted the best for them in this life, but more importantly, Job wanted them to experience a relationship with God.

He also lost his future hope. There would be no continuation of his lineage without children. No one would be left to care for him and his wife in their old age. No one to bury them when the time came.

Troubled

To further this tragic experience, Job was afflicted in his flesh. Boils appeared all over his body producing pain and agony on top of his anguish. A passage from chapter 2 tells the story of the genesis his troubles.

"All right do with him as you please," the LORD said to Satan. "But spare his life." So Satan left the LORD's presence, and he struck Job with terrible boils from head to foot. Job scraped his skin with a piece of broken pottery as he sat among the ashes. His wife said to him, "Are you still trying to maintain your integrity? Curse God and die." But Job replied, "You talk like a foolish woman. Should we accept only good things from the hand of God and

never anything bad?" So in all this, Job said nothing wrong.[20]

The physical suffering Job endured compounded the emotional and spiritual anguish he experienced at the loss of all he worked for and his children whom he loved. It is hard for a person to praise God when the body is hurting. The Lord created man with a connection between spirit, soul, and body. Each one affects the other.

It is easy to give in to the pain and allow self-pity to take hold of our mind when we do not feel well. Job had reason to doubt the faithfulness of God and fall into depression. He made a choice to believe in the kindness of His good God.

Many people live with physical maladies. Some have terminal illnesses while others have debilitating disabilities. Whether the sickness is cancer, cystic fibrosis, ALS, or allergies, it can be hard to see beyond our physical discomfort to see the goodness

---

[20] Job 2:6-10 NASB

of God. The struggle is real for all who battle sickness of any type. Our spiritual well-being can be shaken by our physical healthiness if we allow it to affect us. It is our choice.

The depth of the turmoil in Job's life is evidenced through the words of his wife. Everything Job suffered, she felt, too. She lost her children before their time and all at once. Any mother would question the benevolence of God after experiencing such trauma.

Allow yourself to feel what these two people were feeling for just a moment. Heartache and heart break, fear, doubt, and frustration filled their minds. When we permit ourselves to contemplate our own reactions if it happened to us, it makes Job's choice to continue faithfully serving God even more amazing. He refused to curse the God that previously brought blessing. The same powerful hand that offered good fortune for the first part of his life now seemed to be against him. Still Job made the conscious *Choice to Rejoice* in his tribulation.

In the midst of his emotional and physical torment, Job was challenged on another side. Three of his best friends heard of the tragedies and grief that had befallen Job. These three men conferred together on how to comfort their mutual friend. They travelled from their different homes to meet together and console their friend Job.

Thirty-five chapters in the book of Job are the discourse between these three "comforters" and Job. I hope when I have trouble, I do not have friends like these men. Even more importantly, I hope when my best friend is facing trial, tribulation, and tragedy that I am not like these men myself.

It is the human condition to assume we know what another person may be experiencing when they are troubled. It is another thing to assume we can know the reason why they are having these trials. The message of this story of Job is only God really knows why things happen. Our own prejudices can cloud our vision.

We can easily forget our purpose in this type of situation is to uplift, encourage and comfort the ones who are hurting. We may allow ourselves to fall into the terrible trap of judgementalism. Our role as friend does not make us judge and jury. We can become a cause of more trouble rather than a source of comfort.

The basis of the presumption of these men is Job is hiding something. The thought that God was using Job to display His own glory never entered their minds. The arguments they used against Job were pious and religious in nature. He was a sinner and proud. The Lord was striking Job's family and those closest to him to punish him. We all have skeletons in the closet. Right?

God's testimony of Job was he is a righteous man who reveres and serves the Lord. Still he endured hardship like no other. Perhaps the point God is making is the cause for our troubles is His business alone. He does not require human assistance. Our friends do. We do.

Some day we may find ourselves in a similar place like Job. We will be looking around for someone to help and comfort us. We will need a companion. I hope they treat us better than we deserve. I hope we can do the same for others when they struggle.

Why is it sometimes difficult to support someone when that person may be doing things with which we disagree? The message of the Gospel can be summed up in the phrase "even while I was still a sinner, Christ died for me."[21] That produces a truly clear image to me. Jesus Christ's love for us all compelled Him to sacrifice His life for our benefit.

The example Jesus set for us was to love those who are troubled. The only judgements he ever pronounced were against those purported to be judges themselves. The self-righteous religious crowd of that day experienced the displeasure and

---

[21] Romans 5:8 personalized

disgust of Jesus on many occasions. Downtrodden and broken-hearted people moved him to tears of compassion.

It is easy to point a finger at these men in the story with disgust. Job's friends were not worse people than most of us. The truth is they were just like many of us today. We must be careful lest we be judged the way we judge others. Let us resolve to comfort others rather than confront them.

Triumph

Job had an encounter with the Lord after the confrontation by his friends. The scripture says "out of the whirlwind"[22] the Lord spoke to Job. That is how Job felt when all was lost. He was in a storm without any reference to night or day or shoreline. He was beaten and battered by the adversary allowed by the hand of God.

---

[22] Job 38:1 NLT

In these two chapters, God reproves and instructs Job for his wavering. The Lord queried Job's understanding comparing the greatness of God to the frailty of a man. The questions left Job without an excuse for complaining and justifying himself. In the end, the Lord asked Job,

"Do you still want to argue with the Almighty? You are God's critic, but do you have the answers?"[23]

Job replied, *"I am nothing—how could I ever find the answers? I will cover my mouth with my hand. I have said too much already. I have nothing more to say."*[24]

The Lord's final discourse with Job led him to respond in humility and repentance.

Then Job replied to the LORD: "I know that you can do anything, and no one can stop you. You asked,

---

[23] Job 40:2 NLT
[24] Job 40:4-5 NLT

'Who is this that questions my wisdom with such ignorance?'

"It is I—and I was talking about things I knew nothing about, things far too wonderful for me. You said, 'Listen and I will speak! I have some questions for you. You must answer them.' I had only heard about you before, but now I have seen you with my own eyes. I take back everything I said, and I sit in dust and ashes to show my repentance."[25]

God was not so generous to the friends of Job. He was not pleased with their judgmental attitudes. He did not appreciate their misrepresentation of His character. God commanded these friends to ask Job to pray for them and offer sacrifices for their repentance. Despite Job's feelings about their ridiculing him for his supposed sinfulness, the man of God prayed for them.

The end of the story asserts that God forgave Job for his failure and blessed him once again. He received

---

[25] Job 42:1-6 NLT

double the fortune he lost to the adversary. God restored his family with three daughters and seven sons to replace the ones lost.

Job lived another 140 years after that awful experience. He lived to see four generations of his offspring. He was not a perfect man, but he did walk in integrity as much as humanly possible. His *Choice to Rejoice* when he lost everything created an everlasting heritage.

It Is Well With My Soul

One of the most well-known hymns of the Christian faith was born out of similar tragic circumstances to the life of Job. It Is Well with My Soul was written by a man who experienced trial, tragedy, trouble, and triumph – just like Job.

Horatio G. Spafford was a prominent lawyer of nineteenth century Chicago. He was a friend and supporter of the great evangelist Dwight L. Moody. Horatio was born in Troy, New York in 1828. He married his wife, Anna Larsen, in 1861. The two lived in Chicago raising a family.

As a well-known Presbyterian elder, Spafford befriended Mr. Moody and supported his revival ministry. Chicago experienced one of the most tragic events of American history during this time.

The Great Chicago Fire of 1871 was catastrophic. This event changed both men forever. Spafford lost most of his wealth and investments to the fire. Moody lost over 300 souls to eternity. More than 100,000 people were homeless. Moody resolved from that time on to never preach the Gospel without offering the hearers an invitation to respond. (Made a common custom around the world today)

That same year, the Spafford's lost their four-year-old son to scarlet fever. On November 22, 1873, his wife and four daughters were traveling by ship to England for a vacation. D.L. Moody was holding evangelistic meetings there. Spafford stayed stateside to work on his business and investments lost in the fire.

Their ship, the Ville Du Havre, was struck by another ship and sunk in the Atlantic. The four girls died in the wreck. Only his wife Anna survived. She telegraphed the message "Saved Alone' to Horatio. On his journey to England to gather his mourning wife, Horatio penned the words to the famous hymn. The story says as he passed over the waters where his daughters died, the peace of God. flooded his soul. These words came out of a heart that was crushed by grief but overwhelmed by the faithfulness of God at the same time.

> "When peace, like a river, attendeth my way,
> When sorrows like sea billows roll;
> Whatever my lot, Thou hast taught me to say,
> It is well, it is well with my soul."

Chapter 5
Awaiting Destiny

The smell of smoke and sweat overpowered the aroma of cooking meat throughout the musty space. A dozen filthy fighters gathered around a campfire waiting their turn at the large pot. Others rested their backs against the coolness of the stone wall from the weariness of the day.

The venison stew was mostly broth, but a few chunks of meat were portioned to each man. Served over barley grain with bread, the meal was mostly filling. Some of the men had not eaten a hot, cooked meal for a week so there was not much griping.

Random chatter echoed off the walls while they wolfed down the meal. Music began to drift from deep within the cave. As it floated to the surface, it drowned out the sound of their wooden utensils scraping against earthen bowls.

All chatter slowly subsided as the men listened to the melody drifting from opening of the cave. A harp accompanied the tenor voice of a man singing. As quietness at the mouth of the cave increased, the men could begin to distinguish the words of the psalmist.

"O deliver me from the deceitful and unjust man! For You are the God of my strength. Why have You rejected me? Why do I go mourning because of the oppression of the enemy?"

"Oh send out Your light and Your truth, let them lead me; Let them bring me to Your holy hill and to Your dwelling places. Then I will go to the altar of God, to God my exceeding joy; and upon the lyre I shall praise You, O God, my God."

"Why are you in despair, O my soul? And why are you disturbed within me? Hope in God, for I shall again praise Him, the help of my countenance and my God."

The solemn tranquility of that moment was a stark contrast to the events of the day. Sounds of shouting soldiers had filled the balmy afternoon air. They pursued the disheveled group of men through the brush and brambles of the hillside overlooking

Judah. Slipping away from their trackers, the men found solace and rest now in the concealed network of Adullam's caves.

An olive-skinned young man with broad shoulders emerged from the dark recesses of the hideout. He was greeted with nods of approval by his followers. A large muscular man twenty years his senior offered him a bowl of stew & bread, so he set his small harp down beside a rock. After being assured all the other men had eaten, he dipped the bread into the broth for a large bite.

Some of the men gathered around him as he finished his meal. Laughter spread through the group when one of them tried to sing and play the harp. His screeching voice was only surpassed by his spasmodic beating on the strings of the harp. Mercifully, one of the others snatched the harp from his hand and shoved the would-be musician hard into some bushes. Some chuckles and a collective sigh of relief signaled their appreciation. A few men clapped when the fallen prankster recovered from the bushes with a grandiose bow to his audience.

The young leader retrieved his harp from the grasp of his friend. He lightly strummed its strings creating a melodious tune that transformed the atmosphere. Admiration and respect for this young psalmist shone from glistening eyes of the most seasoned soldiers. His music always brought a sense of the presence of the Almighty into their stronghold.

This mighty young warrior had won over the hearts of hardened men. Spear, sword, and sling were his armament against physical enemies. His bravery and cunning in battle were beyond reproach. Now, his dulcet voice singing praises to the Lord was an even more powerful weapon.

Unseen demons of darkness fled the labyrinth as his victorious praises spurred the angels of heaven into invisible combat. Their angelic brightness expelled all darkness. It was like heaven on earth for the moment.

Rise and Fall

David of Bethlehem is one of the most prominent characters of the Bible. He was the first strong monarch of the nation of Israel. His lineage is causally linked to the birth of Jesus Christ. Many of his psalms of praise are recorded for us to get a glimpse into his heart and his relationship with the Lord Most High. All other kings to follow were measured by the glory of King David.

The legendary conquest of the giant Goliath by the young shepherd is one of the highlights of his life. The tale of this great conflict has been used as an illustration of triumphing against overwhelming odds. Songs were written to declare his greatness.

His subsequent rise to become leader of God's people and armies was surprising. His own brothers thought he was just a young kid eager for fame and glory. Few understood the passion for the Lord burning within his soul. The young servant boy,

David, became a great commander and ruler, uniting all of Israel under God's leadership.

In the midst of all his success, David was not perfect. On one occasion, King David abused his authority and forced a woman to come to the royal palace to have sex with him. This extra-marital affair with Bathsheba began the darkest episode of his life. He betrayed the Lord, his people, and his friends. She was the wife of Uriah, one of his comrades and commanders in his army.

David compounded his sin even more when Bathsheba informed him of her pregnancy. He ordered his troops to withdraw from her husband in the heat of battle. Uriah's death was a murder disguised as tragedy to cover up for the King's great transgression.

Serving in Obscurity

Like many important historical figures, David's life started out in relative obscurity. He was the youngest of eight sons of Jesse of Bethlehem in the territory of Ephraim. It is easy to get lost in the hustle of a large family. In those days, the first-born son received a double inheritance and the role of patriarch after the father's death. There was not much left for the eighth son.

During his early years, David served his father by tending the family's flocks of sheep. These years of solitude and service were crucial to the development of his character. David performed his tasks every day even when no one was watching or supervising him. He cared for the sheep like they were his very own. He learned responsibility and dependability.

The hours of solitude gave him time to become intimate with God. Alone in the pastures and hillsides, David experienced God's presence in ways most of us will never know. The psalms attributed to him reveal his passion for the Lord. Each one declares his understanding of the greatness and glory of God. The Lord truly was his shepherd. Here in seclusion David developed contentment and faith.

David also had countless hours and days to sharpen his skills with both the harp and his slingshot. He practiced until he was an expert. His music brought relief to the tormented. With his trusty sling and a few small smooth tones, he brought down a giant.

David was prepared for both spiritual and physical battle because he developed his skills while alone in the fields and forests. While other boys played, he practiced slinging stones against imaginary foes. David's courage helped him to face real lions and bears in the pastures. These were actual dangers to him and his sheep.

He was anointed by the Prophet Samuel to become King of Israel while still a youth serving in his father's fields. Samuel arrived at Jesse's home, directed there by the Lord to find the new king chosen by God. David was not the first choice by his father. He was actually forgotten and overlooked.

Samuel recognized the difference in this young man as soon as the two met. It was not his physique that distinguished David from his brothers. There was an intangible difference in him that Samuel understood.

David did not look like much to his brothers. Jesse overlooked his youngest son because he was so far down the list. The prophet Samuel rejected the eldest son, Eliab. The Lord warned him not to be swayed by age or appearance. Abinadab, Shammah, and four other sons of Jesse passed by the prophet. Each one was rejected.

God could see what no one else could. He was looking for a man who would be wholly His. The Lord saw the soul of a warrior and worshipper. That is what He revealed to Samuel there at Jesse's home.

David's obscurity did not stop him from serving God. In fact, it was the catalyst of his spiritual growth. He learned persistence and fostered an excellent spirit. Even before he fought giants or sat on the throne, David learned the principle of making a *Choice to Rejoice* while serving in obscurity. It was a lesson that would be put to the test many times in his life.

Stuck in a Cave

After his victory over Goliath the giant, things happened fast for young David. He was immediately given command of the army. He was rewarded with the daughter of King Saul in marriage. Jonathan, Saul's son, and heir to the throne, became his best friend and supporter. David's rise to the top was swift and spectacular. Even his older brothers reluctantly served him now.

The same could be said for his fall from the King's good graces. Once the Israelites began to laud David's victories above those of Saul, it was a matter of time for jealousy to take root. No sovereign will allow one of his generals to receive more glory than the king. Saul became resentful toward his young commander and son-in-law. Envy rapidly became trepidation about losing the people's respect and a hatred for David.

On two occasions, Saul tried to kill David by hurling a javelin at him while they dined in the palace. The thud of the spearhead in the wall was a wakeup call to David. It was time to make his exit. The intensity of animosity burned so fiercely that Saul also threw a spear at his son Jonathan when he questioned his father. No one was safe from Saul's wrath. He threatened both his son and daughter if they attempted to help David. There was no safe spot from the raging sovereign until this stealer of hearts David was gone.

David narrowly escaped capture on many occasions. He escaped from the palace under cover of darkness. There was no time for goodbyes or even to gather his weapons. David fled the country to live with his enemies the Philistines for a while.[26] God blessed him with favor everywhere he traveled.

---

[26] 1 Samuel 27:1-4 NLT

There were many nights that he hid in the hills and caves of Judah. He was constantly moving and on the run. His brothers and many other men who were disenfranchised came to follow him. The former commander of legions was now the leader of a ragged troop of 400 men. They covertly pillaged the enemy strongholds and lived off of the spoils.

Avoiding capture by Saul and providing for his men became David's goal. There were opportunities to take Saul's life twice, but David refused. Hiding in the caves from the wrath of a mad king was complicated. But he knew that to touch the anointed one of God, no matter how crazy that person may be, was asking for more trouble.

David was a great leader of men. He carried the burden for his people as well as the concern for his own life. David's *Choice to Rejoice* in spite of these difficult circumstances was revealed by his actions.

"David was greatly distressed; for the people spake of stoning him, because the soul of all the people was grieved, every man for his sons and for his daughters: but David encouraged himself in the LORD his God."[27]

There are times when despair and depression may darken our hearts and minds just like the walls of a damp cave. Trouble may seem to be around every bend in the path. Tension from within and turmoil without can push us to the brink of surrender. Those times can break us. They can also be the experiences that catapult us to new heights if we see the cave experience as an opportunity to lift up a banner of praise. David was stuck in a cave physically, but he never allowed those walls to crush his hope in God.

What can we do when stuck in a situation that seems hopeless? There are several choices available to each

---

[27] 1 Samuel 30:6 KJV

of us, but they fall into a few main categories. The choice we make determines the rest of our story.

We can run. Flight is always a choice. The simplest thing to do when stuck in a bad job or unhappy in marriage, is run away. We may know it is not the right decision, but it just feels easier. Divorce is sometimes a way of running from our cave. There can be legitimate and good reasons for divorce. Today it is mostly just easier to get out than figure it out. Running from an inconvenient situation may doom us to repeat the same experience in another way since we did not learn the first time.

Running can include anything that helps us escape from the feelings of aloneness and vulnerability. Substance abuse is a type of running away. It most often is the result of not dealing with a challenging time in our life. To feel nothing through use of drugs, alcohol, sex, or gambling is a choice. Many people use them to escape their invisible cave.

Another choice is we can give up. David had many opportunities to just let Saul catch him. There were days of hunger, pain, and complaining by his followers that probably made this a viable option. Throwing in the towel in defeat can be easier than continuing to fight but very costly. David's life would have ended if he surrendered to the mad king.

Scores of people choose option three. We can fight. How different would our feelings toward David be if he pulled the javelin from the wall and threw it back at Saul? He may have felt better and even been justified, but the course of his life would have become so different.

David had opportunities to kill Saul more than once. Taking matters into our own hands may feel right and justified sometimes but it also establishes patterns. What is to stop someone from killing King David if the anointed young David killed King Saul? The cycle of fighting would possibly go on forever.

David avoided conflict with Saul out of respect for his position. He did not just run away in fear or because it was easier. Saul was appointed by God to the throne of Israel. It was actually much more difficult. He did not give up. He chose not to raise his hand against Saul even when spurred on by his closest friends. David lived by his belief in the principle that God will not honor the man who touches God's anointed servant.

The blessing of God was on David's life because he chose the harder way. He was not ruled by his emotions or the desires of others. In those caves, David worshipped the Lord and cried out to Him alone for help. God made the way of escape when David put on the garment of praise for the spirit of heaviness.[28]

Waiting for Destiny

David knew his time would come. From the day that Samuel anointed him to be king, there was always a

---

[28] Isaiah 61:3 NIV

sense of purpose and destiny. He did not fully experience that destiny for many years. Serving in Saul's palace and then his army brought him from adolescence to adulthood. He was on the run in the wilderness for years. Even after the tragic deaths of Saul and Jonathan, his rule was only partly received by the people.

At the age of thirty, David returned to Judah from Philistia. He became king of all Judah at that time. One of Saul's remaining sons was made king over the ten tribes of Israel. It was about seven more years and many more conflicts before David became king over the entire united nation.

This is important. David was hindered for almost a decade before stepping just partly into the role God promised him. At the age of thirty-seven, finally David was allowed to become everything God had spoken to him while a young shepherd. He had waited patiently for the Lord to open the door for him to step into his destiny.

It would have been easy to rush in and take it, but he refused to allow himself that privilege. He had to wait for his time to come to fruition. Man's timeline seldom lines up with the plan of God. David trusted God would make a way when there seemed to be no way.

Waiting on the Lord is one of the great themes of the psalms penned by David. That thought is expressed through most of his writings. It is probably the greatest of all the lessons David learned. There is more to waiting than just sitting around in idleness. It is an activity of worship by declaring God is in control of our times. It is an attitude of perseverance even when facing difficult circumstances.

There is a wealth of knowledge and inspiration we can glean from David's worshipful waiting for the Lord. He displayed an attitude that God cherishes in the heart of His followers. No greater declaration of faith speaks so loudly to the Lord like a believer waiting patiently for Him to move.

Let your heart be encouraged even when you serve in obscurity. Maybe you are stuck in a cave or waiting for the Lord to fulfill His word to you. Do not give in to anxiety and frustration. This too is part of God's plan.

We can learn another principle from David. He did not wait for someone to come along and lift him up. No prayer chains were formed in his behalf. He boldly made the *Choice to Rejoice*. David was a warrior. He was also a passionate worshipper. The two really do go hand in hand.

You have the power to do the same. It is your decision. Encourage yourself in the Lord like King David.

The following scriptures are a few passages from some of the Psalms written by David. Some of them may have been penned while hiding in a cold dark cave. May the Lord give you strength to wait patiently for His destiny for your life.

To You, O LORD, I lift up my soul. O my God, in You I trust, do not let me be ashamed; Do not let my enemies exult over me. Indeed, none of those who wait for You will be ashamed Those who deal treacherously without cause will be ashamed.[29]

Do not let me fall into their hands. For they accuse me of things I have never done; with every breath they threaten me with violence. Yet I am confident I will see the Lord's goodness while I am here in the land of the living. Wait patiently for the Lord. Be brave and courageous. Yes, wait patiently for the Lord.[30]

We wait in hope for the Lord; he is our help and our shield. In him our hearts rejoice, for we trust in his holy name. Let Your lovingkindness, Oh Lord, be upon us, for we have hoped in You.[31]

---

[29] Psalm 25:1-3 NASB
[30] Psalm 27:12-14 NASB
[31] Psalm 33:20-22 NASB

Rest in the Lord and wait patiently for Him; Do not fret because of him who prospers in his way, Because of the man who carries out wicked schemes.[32]

And now, Lord, for what do I wait? My hope is in You.[33]

I waited patiently for the Lord; And He inclined to me and heard my cry. He brought me up out of the pit of destruction, out of the miry clay, and He set my feet upon a rock making my footsteps firm. He put a new song in my mouth, a song of praise to our God; Many will see and fear and will trust in the Lord.[34]

My bones suffer mortal agony as my foes taunt me, saying to me all day long, "Where is your God?" Why, my soul, are you downcast? Why so disturbed

---

[32] Psalm 37:7-9 NASB
[33] Psalm 39:7 NASB
[34] Psalm 40:1-3 NASB

within me? Put your hope in God, for I will yet praise him, my Savior, and my God. [35]

But as for me, I am like a green olive tree in the house of God; I trust in the lovingkindness of God forever and ever. I will give You thanks forever, because You have done it, and I will wait on Your name, for it is good, in the presence of Your godly ones. [36]

O God, You are my God; I shall seek You earnestly; my soul thirsts for You, my flesh yearns for You in a dry and weary land where there is no water. Thus I have seen You in the sanctuary, to see Your power and Your glory. Because Your lovingkindness is better than life, my lips will praise You. So I will bless You as long as I live; I will lift up my hands in Your name. My soul is satisfied as with marrow and

---

[35] Psalm 42:10,11 KJV
[36] Psalm 52:8,9 NASB

fatness, and my mouth offers praises with joyful lips.[37]

I wait for the Lord, my whole being waits, and in his word, I put my hope.[38]

The Lord favors those who fear Him, those who wait for His lovingkindness.[39]

---

[37] Psalm 63:1-4 NASB
[38] Psalm 130:5 NIV
[39] Psalm 147:11 NASB

The Troublemaker

The man we know today as Nelson Mandela was born in an obscure village in South Africa July 18, 1918. His parents named him Rolihlahla in his native language of Xhosa. The literal translation of his name is "pulling the branch of a tree." The more common usage of it by his people is "troublemaker." Later, he was re-named Nelson by his adoptive parents so he might fit into the white world of apartheid. He spent twenty years of his life in the peaceful resistance against this system. Apartheid was racism and domination of his native people. It was instituted by the British in their colonization of south Africa.

In 1961, he changed his tactics to armed resistance and activism against the government. He was put in prison in November 1962 to serve five years for leading national workers strike.

While still incarcerated, he and ten other anti-apartheid leaders were tried and convicted by a court of all white people in 1963. They were sentenced to life in prison for crimes against the government including sabotage.

After spending 27 years in prison for holding to his convictions, Mandela was finally released by the new president of South Africa, Frederik W. de Klerk. His release from prison signaled the end of the rule of apartheid in South Africa. In 1993, Nelson Mandela was elected the first black president of South Africa.

*While alone in the dark and silence of his prison cell, Mandela wrote his autobiography, Long Walk to Freedom. He learned the power of choosing to live a life of joy in spite of what others may do to him. He made **The Choice to Rejoice**. His life changed a nation and touched millions of people around the world.*

Challenges

"Difficulties break some men but make others."

Life

What counts in life is not the mere fact that we have lived. It is what diffcrence we have made to the lives of others that will determine the significance of the life we lead."

127

Chapter 6
A Deeper Revelation

The prisoner stared through the opening in the wall above his head. He could see wasps of smoke floating across the pale blue heavens. The stench of burning wood and human flesh filled the cell. A whiff of boiling olive oil occasionally crowded out the other rancid smells.

The door of the cell was pushed open by the jailer. Two large Roman soldiers of the Praetorian Guard enter. They escorted the prisoner down the long shadowy corridor up into the blazing sunlight. He was welcomed by the cheers of Rome's elite citizenry. Only here is the public execution of a prisoner cause for celebration.

He stood before them surrounded by more guards. Young men shouted obscenities at him while older men and women smiled in approval. The guards propelled him forward into the forum.

A group of boys ran to the stone barrier separating spectator from participants. They waved to the soldiers in celebration of their triumph. Two of the older boys threw rotten onions at the prisoner to the delight of the crowd.

As the man's eyes grew accustomed to the brightness, he saw the fires that filled his cell with smoke and odors of carnage and death. The charred bodies of his brothers in service to Christ were still burning on wooden crosses. There were at least ten he counted.

At the far end of the piazza, two lions wrestled in a cage. They waged a gruesome battle of tug-of-war with the corpse of a believer. Soldiers lounged beside the cage and wagered on which beast would win the conflict.

The guards ushered this final prisoner to the center of the forum to a raised wooden platform. A single wooden plank extended from the platform high over a boiling cauldron. This was the source of the fragrance of olive oil he smelled in his cell.

The guards walked him up the plank to the top of the platform. A young herald read a list of his crimes. Treason against Rome and the Emperor Domitian. Spreading heresies among the people. Lecturing against worshiping the gods of Rome. The sentence was death. The instrument of execution was he would be boiled alive in oil.

He stared into the cauldron. The guard prodded him forward onto the beam. The heat from the oil seared the soles of his bare feet. The soldier stopped because the heat was too intense. He continued to push the condemned man with his spear. Inching ever further, he came to the end of the beam. The crowd grew silent for the moment of anticipation. A final push from his guard sent him falling into the boiling vat.

Cheers rose from the multitudes assembled there. Some arose from their high perches to catch a glimpse of the boiling man. The din of their applause filled the stadium and flooded out into the streets below. Then something no one could have imagined happened. A collective gasp of breath filled the stadium. Finally the ovations subsided, and the crowd quieted.

John jolted awake, startled by his dream. It took a few moments for his eyes to become accustomed to the darkness. He slowly gained his senses and recognized the cave that now was his cell. The aged apostle slowly sat up against the wall of his grotto and looked around.

This had been his home for a while now. His dream was more than a dream. It was the memory of a great miracle of personal deliverance. He was banished to this island cave on Patmos as his sentence. He was hidden away from public view. It was the only way authorities knew to suppress the aftermath of the event that rattled all of Rome.

John placed a broken branch on the fading coals and stoked up a small fire. The warmth felt good to his aging bones. Standing by the fire he glanced at his makeshift calendar on the wall marking the days. He was in his fifth season alone on this solitary island. By his best account, it was the Lord's day.

He walked to the mouth of the cave and gazed into the morning mist. The salty breeze of the Aegean Sea blew his white beard into his face momentarily. Lifting his hands to heaven, the aged disciple offered up his morning praises to the Lord. The presence of the Holy Spirit filled his heart with joy as he worshipped. The sound of the wind in the trees and the waves slapping the shore was his orchestra.

The peace of that moment was broken by a booming voice from the mouth of the cave. John was startled back to the present. He heard, "Write in a book everything you see, and send it to the seven churches in the cities of Ephesus, Smyrna, Pergamum, Thyatira, Sardis, Philadelphia, and Laodicea."

John turned back from the opening. He saw the one speaking to him. The booming voice belonged to the risen Savior, Jesus Christ. John collapsed on the ground. The Lord himself revealed things too awesome and fearful and wonderful for the mind of any man to comprehend.

John, the Revelator

John is a fitting example of one who learned to rejoice in the midst of tribulation. He was the last of the twelve select Disciples of Christ to die. Peter, James and all the others were martyred for Christ. Rome made every attempt to make John one of those as well, but Christian legend says John could not be killed by boiling oil. He miraculously walked out alive.

He spent his remaining days hidden away from the public in solitary confinement on the Isle of Patmos. Rome could not allow a living miracle and witness to Christ's resurrection to walk the streets. He had to be silenced since he did not die. The embarrassment would be too great.

The Revelation John received while there alone on the island is the only prophetical writing included in the canon of the New Testament. It is a foretelling of the last day events planned out by God. These happenings will culminate in the complete overthrow of evil and establishment of God's kingdom over all the earth. The truths revealed to him are beyond amazing.

Boanerges

Jesus encounters John and his brother James while he is traveling through Galilee. The two men are at work on their fishing boat when Jesus calls them to follow him in ministry. This was probably not their first meeting with Jesus. It was not simply by chance either.

We know that Andrew, Simon Peter's brother was a disciple of John the Baptist. The Gospel account states that he first introduced Peter to Jesus.[40] Andrew and Peter were also partnering with James and John in the fishing trade. The brothers spent a lot of time together in their work.[41]

Most of the accounts of the personal interactions of Jesus with his disciples are revealed in the gospel attributed to John. He always refers to himself as a disciple but never by personal pronoun in his writings. The story was always about the Christ. Most scholars believe John was the other follower of John the Baptist introduced to Jesus. John was listed as one of the early disciples of Christ. He was from the city of Bethsaida, along with Peter, Andrew,

---

[40] Luke 5:10 NLT
[41] Mark 1:29 NASB

Philip, and Nathaniel.[42] He and his brother had a couple of encounters with Jesus that reveal a little of their agenda and character. The nickname "Boanerges" means "sons of thunder." It was given to them after they expressed their desire to call down fire from heaven on the village of Samaria.[43] The name was not flattering. It was probably a mild rebuke for their hot tempers.

John also attempted to stop some other followers of Jesus from casting out demons.[44] These people were not part of the twelve disciples chosen by Jesus. He asked the Master for permission but was denied. John may have been trying to protect the integrity of Jesus' ministry, but it also revealed some of the pride in his heart.

---

[42] John 1:35-50 NLT
[43] Luke 9:51-56 NIV
[44] Mark 9:38-39 NASB

In another instance, Salome[45], the mother of the James and John, requested favoritism for her sons from Christ. One of the Gospel accounts shows it differently. It has James and John asking Jesus for the places of honor in his kingdom. This request did not set well with the other disciples. They all felt disrespected by James and John. It exposed some of the worldly ambition still in James' and John's hearts. Jesus was not offended by it. The other disciples clearly were offended. Jesus used it as another opportunity to teach about the difference between the kingdoms of men and the kingdom of heaven.

Both James and John later became patriarchs of the first century church. Both men were powerfully used by God as evangelists and leaders in the early church. John was the only one of the disciples not martyred for the faith. The Lord surely changed their hearts.

---

[45] Mark 10:35-40 NLT & Matthew 20:22-24 NLT

One of the Three

Throughout the gospels, James and John are listed along with Peter as Jesus' closest friends and disciples. Most Biblical scholars believe they were all present at the first miracle performed by Jesus.[46] He turned gallons of water into wine at a wedding feast in Cana. This event served as their introduction to His ministry. It had a powerful effect on them. They all left their lives and businesses when called to follow the Christ.

They were the only disciples allowed in the room to witness the miracle of the resurrection Jairus' daughter.[47] It may have been to demonstrate His power over death. It did that. It may have also opened their eyes to need for faith when doing the works of God. Whatever the reason, the three men had a special relationship with Christ.

---

[46] John 2:1-12 NLT
[47] Luke 8:41-56 NASB

The three of them were the only ones allowed to see Jesus transformed into his heavenly glory.[48] Jesus and the Twelve were passing through the district of Caesarea Philippi on his final journey to Jerusalem. He had spoken to them of His impending death. He also prophetically declared that there were some of those disciples who would not die before seeing Him in His heavenly glory.[49] It was six days later when Christ took only these three men to a mountaintop for prayer. There on the mountain, Jesus was changed before their very eyes. They saw Him in all of His magnificent splendor as King of heaven and earth. He revealed to them the glory hidden from others.

Finally, these three were called apart from the other disciples while in the Garden of Gethsemane. There Jesus wept great drops of blood before his impending crucifixion.[50] He reproved them for falling asleep at the time of His greatest need. Even in personal

---

[48] Matthew 17:1-13 NASB
[49] Matthew 16:28 NLT
[50] Matthew 26:36-46, Mark 14:32-42, & Luke 22:40-46 NLT

disappointment, He still loved them. Jesus demonstrated an exclusive relationship with these three men.

The trio was not better morally or smarter than the others. This was demonstrated throughout their interactions with Christ in the gospel accounts. There was anger, frustration, fear, doubt, and pride displayed in them just like the rest of the disciples. Just like it is in us.

The logical explanation is Jesus chose them to witness these greatest events in His life for them to see him as He really is, the Son of God. There were lessons about His kingdom that could only be explained in a personal way. These men all became the great pillars of the early church. The unique relationship they experienced with Christ up close and personal equipped them for their future ministry roles.

It can also be interpreted from many of the passages that Jesus depended on these men. While on earth, Jesus was a human being like the rest of us except born without the sin nature. He still exhibited a normal need for companionship and fellowship.

It may also be assumed that he needed their faith at times. In the raising of Jairus' daughter, all those with doubt were expelled from the room. Somehow, they had faith even though they had never witnessed such a miracle before. The only thing that stopped Jesus from performing any miracle while on earth was unbelief.[51] Surely the trio assisted Jesus with their faith as they witnessed the miraculous.

There were also times when Jesus expressed displeasure with them when they failed to assist him. As stated previously, Jesus requested his three closest friends to pray with Him in His hour of greatest need in the Garden. As He went apart from

---

[51] Matthew 13:58; Mark 6:5-7, & Mark 16:14 NASB

them to pray alone, the three mighty men fell asleep while praying. Even after a second request to stay awake with Him, Peter, James, and John fell asleep again. Meanwhile, Judas led soldiers into the Garden to arrest Jesus. The temptation to give into their fleshly desire and need for sleep was a failure that all three carried throughout their lives. It changed them forever.

John was one of these three closest friends of Jesus. He saw and heard things only the other two knew about. All of these events were used by God in developing John into the great man of God he would become. In the upper room Passover celebration, John referred to himself as "the disciple whom Jesus loved."[52] He was unique among even Jesus' closest companions.

John was the lone disciple who remained at the cross of Jesus during his crucifixion. All the other

---

[52] John 13;23 NLT; John 19:26 NLT

disciples, including Peter and James, deserted him. He watched as his friend and mentor died a horrible death at the hands of Roman soldiers. The Christ gave John a great responsibility even as he died. He was the one Jesus entrusted with the care of Mary, His mother, after His death.

The Pillar

In the accounts of the early church recorded in the writing of Luke in his Acts of the Apostles, John is listed as one of the leaders of the Jerusalem church. He is called a "pillar" of the church by the Apostle Paul.[53] He is a foundational member to the establishment of this new work called "the Way."[54] John's leadership was instrumental to the existence of the church as we know it today.

Peter and John were the disciples used by God to produce an amazing miracle in Jerusalem. After

---

[53] Galatians 2:9 NIV
[54] Acts 9:2 NLT; Acts 19:20-23 NLT

Pentecost and the baptism of the Holy Spirit, there was a buzz around the church and the men of God. The notoriety did not distract them from the fellowship and communion with God learned through Jesus. They continued their daily routine of worship in the temple. The men were content to worship the Lord. Ambition had finally lost its hold on them.

One day, while entering the temple for their regular time of prayer and worship, the two were confronted with an opportunity. They met a man impoverished by his physical disabilities. It was customary for the poor and needy of that day to station themselves strategically outside the temple. Here the poor waited to receive from the beneficent followers of God.

The story says this place was this man's customary position. On this day, when he requested alms of Peter and John, he received so much more. They did not simply give him money. He was completely healed by the power of Christ. The lame man was empowered to leap and dance on limbs that had never walked before.

This miracle created much rejoicing and quite a stir in Jerusalem. The man was bounding and praising all over the courtyard. Peter used the opportunity to preach to the crowds drawn to the see the miracle man. Hundreds of people heard the message of Christ through this occasion.

This miracle brought the first conflict to the new-birthed church. Peter and John were overrun by crowds of worshippers wanting to see the man known to many as a beggar with disabilities. The Jewish leaders were disturbed by the miracle and the preaching of Peter.[55]

The two disciples were arrested by temple guards and put in jail for the night. John and Peter were brought

---

[55] Acts 4:2 NLT

before the Jewish council to explain their actions. The healed beggar was dragged to court as well.

The two preachers refused to stop proclaiming the resurrection of Jesus. It was confounding to the temple leaders because of the power of the great miracle. They could not possibly deny something great had happened. The beggar with disabilities was well known in the city. Every person entering the Temple had passed him there begging at the door for years. He now stood on two healed legs in their presence rejoicing in his new life.

John is not referenced specifically in their next encounter with the Jewish Law. It says the apostles were arrested.[56] Because of their continued refusal to obey the Jewish leaders, they were beaten and released. Even this could not stop their preaching of the Good News. It actually emboldened them to preach more avidly than ever.

---

[56] Acts 5:18,40

The early church blossomed under the leadership of Peter and the Apostles. John was there at the forefront of the greatest movement of God ever known. His role was as important as any of the other eleven, including Peter.

The Revelator

According to history, John was the youngest of the original disciples chosen by Jesus and the last of the twelve apostles to die. All of his friends and colleagues in ministry had suffered martyrs' deaths but he remained. The Romans tried to extinguish John's light as well. According to the early Christian writer and polemicist Tertullian, John was persecuted under the Roman government of Emperor Domitian. It was said he was taken to a large stadium to be executed by being boiled alive in a large vat of oil. John was unharmed when the execution did not succeed. The story says all in attendance who witnessed the miracle were converted to Christianity.

John was then banished to the small island of Patmos. There no one would know his fate and the legend of his escape from death would soon fade from memory. It was on the isle of Patmos the elderly exiled John received his prophetic message about the end of the age. We call it the Revelation. In this revelation, the Lord himself disclosed things to come to John too wonderful and awesome for the mind of man to comprehend.

We do not know for sure how he died. We can get a glimpse of his changed perspective through this writing. After years of service, hardship, suffering and banishment, the words of John in the first chapter tell us all we need to know about his transformation.

I, John, your brother and companion in the suffering and kingdom and patient endurance that are ours in Jesus, was on the island of Patmos because of the word of God and the testimony of Jesus. On the Lord's Day I was in the Spirit, and I heard behind me a loud voice like a trumpet, which said: "Write on a scroll what you see and send it to the seven churches: to Ephesus, Smyrna, Pergamum, Thyatira, Sardis, Philadelphia and Laodicea." I turned around to see the voice that was speaking to me. And when I turned, I saw seven golden lampstands, and among the lampstands was someone like a son of man, dressed in a robe reaching down to his feet and with a golden sash around his chest. The hair on his head was white like wool, as white as snow, and his eyes were like blazing fire. His feet were like bronze glowing in a furnace, and his voice was like the sound of rushing waters. In his right hand he held seven stars, and coming out of his mouth was a sharp, double-edged sword. His face was like the sun shining in all its brilliance. When I saw him, I fell at his feet as though dead. Then he placed his right hand on me and said: "Do not be afraid. I am the First and the Last. I am the Living One; I was dead, and now look, I am alive for ever and ever! And I hold the keys of death and Hades. "Write, therefore, what you have

seen, what is now and what will take place later.
Revelation 1:9-19 NLT

On the Lord's day, John was in the Spirit. What an awesome testimony of the man of God. Who knows if he would have received the Revelation if he chose to be "in the flesh" on the Lord's Day? What if he were complaining to God about his lot or even blaming the Lord for failure to take care of him? Those feelings can be understood. Many of us would not blame him for having those sentiments. We will never know. John made the better choice instead. He made *The Choice to Rejoice*.

The Spiritual Man

Watchman Nee is one of Christianity's most controversial figures. His writings and teachings of the early twentieth century have challenged the thoughts of millions of believers.

Nee was not formally educated, and he sourced his teachings from various writings, teachers, and his personal studies of the Bible. Some sincere believers call his writings into doubt. Others, equally earnest, express gratitude for the freshness of his teachings that make Christ the center of all.

No one can call into question his faith or commitment. Watchman Nee died in a Communist prison cell in 1972 after suffering more than twenty years for preaching the gospel. He was imprisoned by the new regime for crimes against the state. Hundreds of his followers were forced to accuse him of these various crimes through intimidation, torture, imprisonment, and death.

No one knows exactly how he died. His body was cremated before anyone could arrive. His family still does not know to the present day.

Brother Nee ministered for over 30 years helping to plant more than 400 churches in mainland China, and another 30 in Malaysia, Taiwan, and southeast Asia. His goal was to teach believers the necessity and pathway to a life of consecration, wholly given to God for His service. His life of brokenness, sickness, and eventual imprisonment for the cause of Christ gave him insights to the revelation of Christ and his body known by very few people before or since.

The Normal Christian Life is one of the most powerful books ever written. It was compiled from a collection of his sermons given while traveling through Europe in 1938. The book expounds on Romans 6 and the reality of the believer living the crucified life of Christ in personal and practical experience.

Nee preached through the many years of hardship brought on by the Japanese in WWII. During the Communist takeover, he continued his work in China. Nee sent his co-workers to Taiwan. His life epitomized a deeper revelation of the Christ.[8]

Nee on Rejoicing
"Towards himself a Christian should have a broken spirit, but towards God it should be one of rejoicing always in Him. He rejoices not for its own sake nor because of any joyful experience, work, blessing or circumstance, but exclusively because God is his center."

Nee on God's Will
"The right attitude is this: that I have my own will, yet I will the will of God."

Nee on the Spiritual Man
"Faith in Christ makes one a regenerated believer; obedience to the Holy Spirit makes him a spiritual believer."

Nee on the Choice to Rejoice
If Christ lives in us, we will rejoice in everything, and we will thank and praise the Lord. We will say, 'Hallelujah! Praise the Lord' forever.

Nee on the Christian Life

"The Christian life from start to finish is based upon this principle of utter dependence upon the Lord Jesus."

Nee on the Work of Christ

"Because the Lord Jesus died on the Cross, I have received forgiveness of sins; because the Lord Jesus rose from the dead, I have received new life; because the Lord Jesus has been exalted to the right hand of the Father, I have received the outpoured Spirit. All is because of Him; nothing is because of me."

His Final Words

"Christ is the Son of God. He died to atone for men's sin, and after three days rose again. This is the most important fact in the universe. I die believing in Christ."

(Found on a handwritten note under a mattress in his prison cell after his death)

Chapter 7
The Finish Line

The deep darkness was instantly illuminated by a piercing brightness no eye could withstand. Rocks quivered and groaned under a heavy weight. The stone walls were no match for the power emanating from within. There He stood erect facing the opening of the cave. It was illuminated by the glory of God surrounding him.

An audible groaning echoed through the inner recesses of the cave. Another loud snap like a mighty limb breaking from a tree followed. Chaotic voices on the outside of the cave quickly vanished as the guards ran away in fear. He moved to the opening of the cave as a massive stone covering the opening was rolled back. The ragged ends of the snapped ropes used to secure the stone fell to the ground. The massive rock came to a stop and the glorious One stepped into the world of the living again.

Angelic beings surrounded the figure as He strode from the once impenetrable cave into the breaking dawn. The glorified figure lifted his hands toward heaven in worship while bathing in the fresh morning air. He turned and looked back at the opening gazing into His former prison cell. Then He vanished into the morning mist.

In the twinkling of an eye, all of heaven erupted in praise. His appearance in the Grand Hall was as sudden as His disappearance into the mist. It was a celebration long awaited. Hosts of cherubic singers belted forth choruses of "Worthy is the Lamb who was slain!" The room overflowed with joy and festivity at the sight of Him. Flashes of light danced around the throne room of heaven to the rhythm of the angelic melodies.

He advanced toward the far end of the palatial room. With each deliberate step toward the Throne, the worshiping spirits fell quiet. Each one bowed low and knelt before Him as he passed. Their joy was now exceeded by His immense holiness and power. Each step brought Him closer to His reward.

All attention was directed to the Father who sat upon the Throne. Complete silence filled the hall. The Father met the gaze of His Son as He drew closer. The Father's eyes beamed with love and appreciation. He motioned with extended left hand toward another Throne on the right side of his own.

The seat was solid gold illuminated with rows of rubies, emeralds, and pearls. The steps leading to the throne flashed a brilliant white with each step. The glorious Son took his place beside the Father.

"Well done, My Son. You have run the race set before you to the finish. Your victory is complete. Death and hell have lost their hold on You. You have done all

that was required of You. You have shown mankind Our love. They can now be freed from the bondage of sin and death as well. Now, enter Your rest as the victor. Take your rightful place beside Me once again."

"Father, I praise You for Your infinite wisdom. I have completed all you have set before me. I have revealed to them the love you have given Me. I rejoice, not that I have suffered, but that suffering has revealed the truth concealed from ages past. No more shadows hidden in sacrifice and offering."

Standing to his feet, the Son revealed his nail-scarred hands. The hall erupted once again as He shouted, "Now My dear children will receive the forgiveness purchased with my own blood. Now they may receive the joy that I possess. Their sins may be washed. Redemption is at hand for all who will believe and receive. My race is done. It is complete. I have crossed the Finish Line."

Joy Through Sorrow

One of the most glorious passages in the Bible is found in the last portion of the letter to the Hebrews. For centuries there has been debate about the authorship of this epistle. The great Apostle Paul was considered by early church leaders to be the writer. Later historians and theologians have considered Luke, the writer of his gospel and Acts, or even Priscilla, a female teacher in the early church.

Despite not having a direct claim to its authorship, this epistle has been considered one of the great theological treatises of all time. It has been accepted as part of the canon of scripture for hundreds of years because of the soundness of the theology presented, the beauty and clarity of the message, and the classical style of the writing. Jesus is presented as the High Priest who has finished God's work of redemption by the sacrifice of His own life.

The following passage describes the Finish Line:

"Therefore, since we are surrounded by such a huge crowd of witnesses to the life of faith, let us strip off every weight that slows us down, especially the sin that so easily trips us up. And let us run with endurance the race God has set before us. We do this by keeping our eyes on Jesus, the champion who initiates and perfects our faith. Because of the joy awaiting him, he endured the cross, disregarding its shame. Now he is seated in the place of honor beside God's throne."[57]

This exhortation was written to encourage believers, but the image of Christ in it is awesome. Jesus was empowered to endure the suffering of the cross and death because of the "joy awaiting Him."

Jesus did not look *at* the cross, but rather ***through*** it.

Jesus did not see a dead end or a stop sign. The cross was a doorway. He saw the Finish Line on the other

---

[57] Hebrews 12:1-3 NLT

side. The final words of Christ from the cross say it all for Him. "It is finished."

There is great satisfaction in finishing a task. There is even more joy when the task is for the betterment of people you love. Jesus was not concerned with finishing the race for His own personal gain or comfort. It was quite the opposite. It cost Him everything.

The joy that waited for Him on the other side is all the people who would choose to follow Him. Jesus was looking through the cross at you and me on the other side. He saw the Father waiting for Him there, too. He was there with arms open wide as Jesus crossed the Finish Line.

This message of joy through suffering was a major part of the teaching of Christ to his disciples. It was difficult for them to understand that the Messiah did not come to establish an earthly kingdom. The customary belief was that the coming Messiah would free them from the political oppression of Rome. He would come to restore the throne of David in Bethlehem.

The disciples were very confused whenever Jesus discussed His death.[58] They simply could not grasp it. It made no earthly sense to them. Jesus rebuked Peter openly when he challenged Him. The claim that Jesus must suffer, and die could not be true.[59]

The account of the Last Supper in John's gospel is both profound and personal. Jesus washed His disciples' feet before dining with them for the last time. He shared His approval and His food with the men who were his closest friends. He spoke to them as companions not pupils.

At the table, Jesus spoke very plainly. He disclosed that one member of their group would betray him. Jesus also told Peter that He knew he would fall away

---

[58] John 14:8-11 NASB; John 16:16-22 NASB
[59] Mark 8:31-33 NLT

and deny knowing Him. The Master did not chastise or criticize him. If anything, He encouraged Peter that there would be a place and a plan for him even after failure and betrayal.

Jesus declared His love for each of them. He exhorted them all to love one another, even as He had loved them. He reassured them with promises of His presence and of the coming of the Comforter, the Holy Spirit. He called them His friends and spoke of his devotion.

Finally, He warned them of many persecutions they would experience because of their belief in Him. The path ahead of them would be difficult. It was now their race to run. Each one would be judged for how they completed their own race. There were no promises of wealth and position. The disciples no longer jockeyed for power in His kingdom. Those days were far behind them now.

Birth Pains

Jesus described another wonderful image of joy received through pain in John 16:16-22.

A little while, and you will no longer see Me; and again a little while, and you will see Me. Some of His disciples then said to one another, "What is this thing He is telling us, 'A little while, and you will not see Me; and again a little while, and you will see Me'; and, 'because I go to the Father'?" So they were saying, "What is this that He says, 'A little while'? We do not know what He is talking about." Jesus knew that they wished to question Him, and He said to them, "Are you deliberating together about this, that I said, 'A little while, and you will not see Me, and again a little while, and you will see Me'? Truly, truly, I say to you, that you will weep and lament, but the world will rejoice; you will grieve, but your grief will be turned into joy. Whenever a woman is in labor, she has pain, because her hour has come; but when she gives birth to the child, she no longer remembers the anguish because of the joy that a child has been born into the world. Therefore you too have grief now; but I will see you again, and your heart will rejoice, and no one will take your joy away from you.

These men were faithful followers. The disciples could not understand when Jesus told them He was leaving. Each one had given up their life to follow Him for three years. Their natural inclination was to go back to their former lives. Jesus knew they needed spiritual strength to continue the work He started. This description of a woman giving birth finally opened their minds to the reality of His impending suffering. This analogy brought clarity.

Childbirth illustrates the process of joy springing forth through suffering. A mother must experience physical pains to bring forth a child into the world naturally. It is extremely taxing and hard on the body. Her shouts of agony, pain, and discomfort are real. They are immediately replaced with waves of rejoicing when the child is delivered. Pain is quickly forgotten once a mother takes her child into her arms the first time.

The disciples were guaranteed to experience the suffering of loss at the cross. They would also feel the liberation of rejoicing because of His resurrection from the dead. The pains of birth through the tomb would bring about new life.

These words Jesus spoke would bring them abundant comfort and support after the Lord's crucifixion. He wanted them to understand His death was not the end but rather the beginning of something new. It would be days and weeks before the full reality of this truth became known to them.

Who Are You Looking For?

On that first Sunday after the crucifixion, Mary Magdalene and the other ladies went to the tomb in the early morning hours. Her wish was to properly prepare His body for burial. Their minds pushed them through the pain. The heartbreak of the previous days settled in like a fog. They were prepared to grieve. They were not prepared to find the gravestone to be rolled away and the tomb empty.

Mary's first thought was that the opponents to Jesus' ministry had taken away the body to disrupt the followers even more. She was heartbroken already and this disappointment was almost too much for her soul to bear. Her broken heart flowed freely down her cheeks into the dirt where she knelt. The women sat there weeping before the open tomb.

They were all surprised when two men appeared in their midst. These were no ordinary men. Their robes shone with the brightness of the sun. It was the words these two angelic beings spoke next that really surprised the grieving ladies.

"Why do you seek the living One among the dead? He is not here, but He has risen. Remember how He spoke to you while He was still in Galilee, saying

that the Son of Man must be delivered into the hands of sinful men, and be crucified, and the third day rise again." [60]

Mary Magdelene ran to get the other disciples and inform them about what she had just witnessed. Peter and John were the first to arrive at the scene. The empty tomb, the grave clothes unoccupied like a cocoon, and the face wrap laid carefully to the side confounded these men.

How could this be? The tomb had been sealed and guarded. Who would have been so bold to do such a thing? Why would anyone want to steal His body? It made no sense to them.

After Peter and John returned to the house, Mary stayed outside the empty tomb. She stepped inside while weeping for her Lord. Moving further into the tomb to see, she was met with the presence of two angels. They spoke to her briefly but still she did not

---

[60] Luke 24:5,6 NASB

understand. Stepping outside the tomb she was met by a man she presumed to be the gardener. The man asked why she was crying. Mary's trembling voice begged him to show her where they had taken the body of her Lord.

Once again, the man questioned her, "Who are you looking for?"[61] This time she recognized His voice. How could this be? Mary realized He was no gardener! He was Jesus, HER RISEN LORD! Her weeping turned to rejoicing in that moment. HE IS RISEN! JESUS IS ALIVE!

Sometimes in the moments of our greatest heartache and disappointment, we lose our focus. We can be so overcome by disappointment and loss that we do not see God in our situation anymore. It is like a fog rolling in that clouds our way forward.

It is easy to fall into the trap of "this is the end." We are simple finite beings. The Lord is infinite and all-

---

[61] John 20:15 NLT

knowing. God is not bound by our end. For Jesus, the grave was just the beginning of His greatest triumph. He finished His race to the glory of God.

He Sees Us

Now, His ministry has changed. The Master no longer walks alongside us. He is seated at the right hand of the Father making intercession for us[62]. Jesus is praying for us as we run our race. All of those who have passed through the Finish Line ahead of us are there watching, too. They cheer us on.

The work of God is now realized through those of us running the race on earth. Jesus is not walking beside us, but He has sent the Holy Spirit to be within us. He set the pace and the course for the rest of us to follow. The Spirit guides us and empowers us to run the course.

This point that He sees us when we struggle is made clear in another experience of the disciples. On the

---

[62] Romans 8:34 NASB

night after the miracle of feeding five thousand people. The Lord and his followers spent the afternoon serving over 5000 people. Jesus healed all who came to Him. The disciples passed out food to the crowds and then picked up the leftovers. They were all exhausted.

The day was not over for them yet. Jesus sent the disciples across the lake on to their next assignment. He spent the night in prayer alone on a mountain.

The disciples were in a boat three to four miles from land. They sailed the boat into the middle of a storm at four in the morning. Jesus *saw* them struggling against the winds and waves. He was praying for them.

The Master knew the men were tired and afraid. Serving the needs of over five thousand hungry people was exhausting. Fighting the winds and waves drained their physical strength. They struggled to see any glimmer of hope or land. In the midst of the night's darkest hour and a raging storm, Jesus came to them walking on water.[63] They did not recognize Him either. Their fear of death in the storm was superseded by their superstition.

Even when we cannot see Him, He sees us. It is not humanly possible to see a small boat four miles out in a large sea in the darkest hours of the morning. It is also impossible for any man to see through a tempestuous storm. That is true.

Jesus sees us in our times of greatest need. He sees us in our struggle and pain and intercedes for us. That too is true.

The end from the beginning

Jesus asks not "what" we are looking for but rather "who" we are looking for. The keys to all of our greatest needs is wrapped up in that answer. When He is standing right before us, do we see Him?

---

[63] Mark 6:45-52 NASB

Jesus sees the end from the beginning. He started at the beginning of the course with finishing as His goal. Although there were a couple of times, He was touched with doubt about the course laid before Him, He never gave up. He never took a shortcut or cut corners. Jesus kept pushing forward even when it was clear to do so would cost His very life.

There is never any real victory accomplished without paying a price. The cost of giving up is much greater than the price of pushing through to the end. No successful runner starts out with the thought of quitting. Pushing through pain is part of the process. Anguish cannot be ignored. It must be conquered. We will have to force ourselves to go beyond anything we ever imagined if we are to finish our race triumphantly.

The Father watches us as we run. The Son cheers us on to the finish. Those who have gone before us fill the heavens with praise. As Jesus ran His race to please the Father and to receive the prize, so should we run our race today to enter into His joy.

*His master said to him, 'Well done, good and faithful servant. You were faithful with a few things; I will put you in charge of many things; **enter into** the **joy** of your master.'*[64]

---

[64] Matthew 25:23 NASB

Chariots of Fire

Running the race was both a physical activity as well as a spiritual metaphor for Eric Liddell. He was one of the fastest sprinters ever. He competed in the Paris Olympics of 1924 for Great Britain. He was also a faithful servant of God who chose a life of missionary service over one of athletic fame.

Eric was born to missionary parents serving in Northern China on January 16,1902. His youth was spent in Scotland where he was educated and participated in athletics. His skill as a rugby player was only surpassed by his running ability. He was a naturally fast sprinter who did not have great form or formal training as a runner.

Eric participated in the 1924 Olympics in Paris as a sprinter on the 100meter team from Scotland. There was a challenge for him beyond physically running the race. The qualifying heats for the 100m were on Sunday. Eric had committed to honor the Lord's commands. He would not participate in any athletic events on Sunday. He won both the 200m and 400m events scheduled on the weekdays following.

Liddell set records in those Olympic Games that were unbroken for twelve years. Before the race, one of the team masseurs handed Eric a handwritten note. It said, "In the old book it says: 'He that honors me I will honor.' Wishing you the best of success always." Eric used the words on that note to stimulate his faith to run.

After the Olympics, Eric returned to Northern China in 1925 to serve the Lord. He revisited his home in Scotland to visit family only twice while serving in China. He married the daughter of Canadian missionaries in 1934. They served together in China. Their union was blessed with three daughters.

In 1941 the British government encouraged the return of all citizens from China. Japan was aggressively expanding into the region. It was precarious for everyone there during that time. Eric remained in China. His pregnant wife Florence returned to England with two daughters. Florence gave birth to Maureen in England. Eric died before she could meet her father.

The last two years of Eric's life were spent as an intern at the Japanese Weihsein Internment Camp. He continued to serve the Chinese people even during interment. He cared for the sick and elderly while also educating the youth. He died in the camp February 21, 1945 from exhaustion and sickness. The prisoners were liberated from the camp 5 months later.

Eric was a living example of running his race well. He lived his life as he ran every race. He always gave every ounce of his strength. With his personal finish line in sight, Eric's last words were "It's complete surrender." He had given all joyfully for the crown awaiting him at the end of his race.

The movie **Chariots of Fire,** *produced in 1981, revolves around the lives of two amazing athletes. Eric Liddell was the Scottish champion. The great English racing competitor, Harold Abraham, was his challenger. The story follows the two runners and contrasts their viewpoints.*

Liddell was ruing for the glory of God. Abrahams, an English Jew, was battling against racial prejudice and injustice for his people. In 1982, the film won the Oscars for Best Picture and Best Original Screenplay.

His Secret to Success

"The secret of my success over the 400 meters is that I run the first 200 meters as hard as I can. Then, for the second 200 meters, with God's help, I run harder."

Eric's response 20 years later, when asked how he managed to keep his fantastic pace with such a curious style. He was speaking to Frank Wright of the Aberdeen Press and Journal.

Second Best

"Many of us are missing something in life because we are after the second best, I put before you what I have found to be the best - one who is worthy of all our devotion - Jesus Christ. He is the Savior for the young and the old. Lord, here I am."

The Goal
"As Christians, I challenge you. Have a great aim - have a high standard - make Jesus your ideal...make Him an ideal not merely to be admired but also to be followed."

God's Plan in Circumstances
"Circumstances may appear to wreck our lives and God's plans, but God is not helpless among the ruins. God's love is still working. He comes in and takes the calamity and uses it victoriously, working out His wonderful plan of love."

Knowing God
"You will know as much of God, and only as much of God, as you are willing to put into practice.

Missionaries
"We are all missionaries. Wherever we go we either bring people nearer to Christ or we repel them from Christ."

"Christ for the world, for the world needs Christ!"

Chapter 8
It is Your Choice Now

The *Choice to Rejoice* is more than a catchy phrase. It is a call to action. Finding joy despite life's circumstances requires faith in the goodness of God. It does not mean that we are free from conflicts or challenges. We face conflict from within our hearts and minds. We also are also faced with pressures from outside circumstances of life. We need to learn how to live with joy.

Joy is not the same as happiness. Happiness is the state of being happy. It is the expression of gladness or cheerfulness. Happy is an emotion. It is based on feelings of pleasure and satisfaction. Happiness can come and go in the blink of an eye.

The two terms are used interchangeably by many people. There is a real distinct difference between the two terms. Joy is not dependent upon the circumstances being favorable. It is not an emotion. Joy is not subject to feelings or sensations.

There is no way that happiness can equal joy and rejoicing since those are commanded and produced from a living relationship with Jesus. For example, we are never happy when we lose a loved one, but we can rejoice when we know that loved one is with the Lord. All of the characters in this book were faced with struggle, loss, grief, and hardship of some type. Each one displayed the power of "*The Choice to Rejoice.*"

Darkness Before the Dawn

The psalmist of Israel, David knew of the *choice to rejoice* hundreds of years before the birth of Christ. He experienced hardship when running from a jealous king wanting him dead. David knew loneliness. He felt the sting of disappointment when betrayed by those he loved.

In the midst of his pain and heartbreak, David expressed great devotion to God. Some of his greatest Psalms were written during those times. These words have helped people through the centuries overcome trials and difficulties. David more than once made the *Choice to Rejoice.*

Sing praise to the LORD, you His godly ones, and give thanks to His holy name. His anger is but for a moment, His favor is for a lifetime. Weeping may last for the night, but a shout of joy comes in the morning. [65]

New Testament Joy

In the New Testament, joy is one of the characteristics listed as "fruit of the Spirit."[66] This is "fruit" in a singular form. There is one fruit with many pieces. The nine character traits listed in that passage are really the evidence of God's life being reproduced within a believer. It results when a person is living under the influence and control of the Holy Spirit.

For illustrative purposes, joy can be compared to one slice of an orange. The orange is singular. Joy is produced simultaneously with the other slices. Since all fruit results from the life of the tree, God compares to the orange tree. The orange in this illustration is love. God's character is love. The other

---

[65] Psalm 30:4,5 NASB
[66] Galatians 5:22,23 NASB

slices are listed in patience, peace, goodness, faithfulness, gentleness, meekness, and self-control. Each one of these traits describes a different facet of God's love. Happiness and joy may be used interchangeable in their everyday use, but their meanings are not exactly the same.

The Joy of the Lord

Jesus demonstrated the presence of joy even when faced with the certainty of death at the hands of sinful men. He never said He was happy about it. He demonstrated to the world how to face adversity with grace. Joy is translated from the Greek word "chara." "Grace is translated from the term "charis." Both qualities emanate from the heart of God.

In His final personal discourses with His twelve chosen disciples, Jesus spoke of the power of joy. While dining with the disciples in celebration of the Passover, Jesus spoke very plainly to them. He spoke very plainly of His great love for them. He demonstrated the humility required to truly be a servant of God when washing each man's dirty feet.

The last words of a dying man are considered to be both telling and important. These final words in the upper room were His instructions for the disciples He loved so much. He knew the task before Him in Jerusalem would be His last and greatest acts as a man. This was His way of preparing His followers for the difficult days ahead.

In John 15, Jesus used the illustration of a vine and the branches to describe their spiritual relationship. Jesus is the vine, the source of life. The believer is a branch totally dependent on that life flowing from the vine. Fruit results from a healthy relationship between the vine and the branches. The one caring for the Vine is the Father. He is the one who prunes branches that they may bear the most fruit possible.

His glory is manifested when each branch bears fruit to the fullest potential. This was one of the final teachings Jesus shared with His disciples. It was especially important to Him.

Once again, Jesus connected joy with love in this teaching.[67] Jesus remained in the love of the Father

---

[67] John 15:9-14 NLT

by obeying His will. He experienced boundless joy. Jesus also imparted immense joy to His Father because of His devotion. Loving obedience results in joy.

The believer does the same when obeying the command of Jesus to love one another. Walking in love and obedience is the action that will free us from selfishness and fear. Real joy is the result. That kind of joy cannot be taken away by anyone or any circumstance. It is an abounding and abiding sense of the pleasure of God.

"I have told you these things so that you will be filled with my joy. Yes, your joy will overflow!"[68]

In the next chapter, John 16, Jesus declares even more explicitly what will happen. He knew of His impending death and sacrifice. The disciples did not apprehend what Jesus told them, even when He spoke so plainly. He did not reprove them for their lack of comprehension. Instead He disclosed to them His understanding for them.

---

[68] John 15:11 NLT

These are the things He disclosed to them. The days ahead would be difficult. The crucifixion would be terrible and traumatic. His sudden death would create instability and doubt. The subsequent resurrection from the dead would be even more astonishing and confusing. Jesus explained there would be days of rejoicing by the world because of His death. He would die a sinner's death. These same events would bring pain, remorse, and grief to His followers.

He also told them that God would turn the tables on those who did not believe. The disciples who grieved would be able to rejoice again because of His resurrection. Those who reveled in His death would rejoice no more. Sorrow would indeed be turned into rejoicing.

"It will be like a woman suffering the pains of labor. When her child is born, her anguish gives way to joy because she has brought a new baby into the world. So you have sorrow now, but I will see you again; then you will rejoice, and no one can rob you of that joy.[69]

---

[69] John 16:21,22 NLT

Rejoice in the Lord

Paul is another of the characters studied in this book. He and Silas displayed great faith when they began to belt out praise songs while on lock-down in prison. They were in a dungeon in Philippi where they made their choice to rejoice. That decision affected those men in jail cells and their jailers, as well. It was the head jailer who took Paul and Silas to his home after the Lord miraculously set them free from their shackles. A church was birthed in Philippi from this experience. That is the power of *"The Choice to Rejoice."*

Later in his life, Paul wrote a personal letter to this same church in Philippi. Many of these people in the church were present when those prison doors flew open and the preachers were set free. They knew the power of rejoicing in tribulation firsthand.

One method for studying the scriptures is perceiving the theme of the writer. Joy is the central theme of the letter to the church at Philippi. The word *"rejoices"*, or forms of it, are used sixteen times in a little more than one hundred verses in four chapters. He must have considered this message to be essential to the Philippian believers. This was the last communication he had with the church for which he cared. Paul, like Jesus, used this last message to express a few of his essential instructions.

"Rejoice in the Lord always; again I will say, rejoice!"[70]

The word rejoice is used twice in this one verse. Both times it is in the imperative mode which means it is a command. Therefore, it is not optional. It is not conditional. It is the expected behavior from one who is a follower of Jesus. This instruction carries the same weight and responsibility as any of the other commands of scripture. There is no excuse allowed.

The qualifier in the verse is "in the Lord." When we are in relationship with Jesus Christ, we have the resources to rejoice no matter what the circumstances. God would never command anyone to do something they were not equipped to accomplish.

---

[70] Philippians 4:4 NLT

Peter's Joy

The Apostle Peter was one of those who lived and learned at the foot of Jesus. He was passionate in life. He was devoted at times and disappointed Christ at other times. There was no doubt about what Peter was thinking because he usually had no problem saying it aloud. Even when he was wrong.

His letters to the followers of Christ had a recurring theme. He reminded these devotees living thirty years after the resurrection of the cost of following Christ. He used the theme of the last days of earth to motivate the church.

Since it was possible that they were living in the last days before Christ's return, Peter implored the people to live holy lives. This holiness should be exemplified in every area of their life. It should affect their personal character, their family and business relationships, and their relationship to the world. He encouraged them to demonstrate their faith in obedience and love.

Because he believed they were alive in the last days, Peter wanted believers to understand what was happening to them. The world that previously rejected Jesus Christ would not receive them either. Living for Christ would be hard. Opposition would come in all types and forms. Their weapon would not be hatred or resistance. It would be joy. It would be loving those who did not love in return. This is the Christ life.

The world understands revenge. *"I don't get mad, I get even"* is the mantra of many people. Society is not equipped to understand people who are rejoicing in the midst of suffering. It does not make sense to the unbeliever. There is no force in Hell capable of stopping the Gospel when it is powered by the joyful heart. The presence of suffering and trouble was to be a sign that they were truly following Christ.

Peter also reminded the disciples the reason Jesus died was so mankind could be saved. Jesus saw through His pain to their salvation and received boundless joy. The goal of believers should be the same. Whatever we experience in this life is nothing compared to the reward received in the next life. We shall doubtless come rejoicing, bringing our sheathes with us.[71]

Peter used the teaching of the final days of earth to provoke them to holy living through fear of judgement. He used love as a motivational tool. He inspired them through the power of association with others experiencing similar hardships. He wanted them to live their best possible life no matter how difficult the experiences each one faced.

Joy is the most powerful weapon available to the believer living in this fallen world. Joy and rejoicing are more than a feeling or an emotion. Joy is not controlled by the circumstances faced by believers, but rather controls the environment around us. "*The Choice to Rejoice*" was and is undefeated by pessimism, fear, and hostility.

Faith is a choice to believe God's word instead of what you can see or feel. You may find yourself facing overwhelming difficulty and hardship. Maybe you feel alone in the dark. Whatever the experience you have, God has given you a wonderful

---

[71] Psalm 126:6 KJV

opportunity. Faith is like a muscle that only grows stronger with exercise. Making the *choice to rejoice* when everything and everyone around you says you should feel sorry for yourself will require great faith.

Today, the choice is yours. No one can or will decide but you. It is a great responsibility we each bear.

"Truly, truly, I say to you, that you will weep and lament, but the world will rejoice; you will grieve, but your grief will be turned into joy." [72]

Therefore, having been justified by faith, we have peace with God through our Lord Jesus Christ, through whom also we have obtained our introduction by faith into this grace in which we stand; and we exult in hope of the glory of God. And not only this, but we also exult in our tribulations, knowing that tribulation brings about perseverance; [73]

---

[72] John 16:20 NASB
[73] Romans 5:2,3 NASB

Finally, brethren, rejoice, be made complete, be comforted, be like-minded, live in peace; and the God of love and peace will be with you". [74]

"...the former proclaim Christ out of selfish ambition rather than from pure motives, thinking to cause me distress in my imprisonment. What then? Only that in every way, whether in pretense or in truth, Christ is proclaimed; and in this I rejoice. Yes, and I will rejoice, for I know that this will turn out for my deliverance through your prayers and the provision of the Spirit of Jesus Christ." [75]

Holding forth the word of life; that I may rejoice in the day of Christ, that I have not run in vain, neither laboured in vain. Yea, and if I be offered upon the sacrifice and service of your faith, I joy, and rejoice with you all.[76]

---

[74] 2 Corinthians 13:11 NASB
[75] Philippians 1:17-19 NASB
[76] Philippians 2:16,17 KJV

See that no one repays another with evil for evil, but always seek after that which is good for one another and for all people. Rejoice always; pray without ceasing." [77]

…who are protected by the power of God through faith for a salvation ready to be revealed in the last time. In this you greatly rejoice, even though now for a little while, if necessary, you have been distressed by various trials, so that the proof of your faith, being more precious than gold which is perishable, even though tested by fire, may be found to result in praise and glory and honor at the revelation of Jesus Christ; [78]

Will you make "The Choice to Rejoice"?

---

[77] 1 Thessalonians 5:16-18 NIV
[78] 1 Peter 1:5-7 NASB

The Last Word

God has given us the unique ability to make choices. We have the freedom to decide many things in this life. He has also given us the responsibility to choose to serve Him. That brings us to accountability for our choices.

"Today I have given you the choice between life and death, between blessings and curses. Now I call on heaven and earth to witness the choice you make. Oh, that you would choose life, so that you and your descendants might live! You can make this choice by loving the LORD your God, obeying him, and committing yourself firmly to him. This is the key to your life."[79]

The Father made His choice. He sent Jesus Christ to be the Savior of the world.[80] Jesus made His choice. He willingly gave His life as a sacrifice for our sins so we could be forgiven.[81] God has made it possible

---

[79] Deuteronomy 30:19,20 NLT
[80] John 3:16 NASB
[81] Romans 5:12-17 NLT

for us to be forgiven and made righteous through Jesus Christ. Now we must choose for ourselves.

You can make that choice to follow Jesus and receive life today by simply praying this prayer:

Lord, I acknowledge my sin to you and ask for your forgiveness. I thank you that you sent Jesus Christ to die on the cross for my sin. Thank You He is risen from the dead to set me free from the power of sin and death. I make the choice today to surrender my own will to follow your will. God, I will live for you from this day forward. I ask for you to save me and be the Lord of my life. Help me to learn to make the right choices every day. I choose life today! Amen.

Made in the USA
Columbia, SC
27 December 2021